'tis a very proud thing to be irish

Borrowed
from

the
O'Driscoll
Library

Cobh

Skibbereen

Céad
míle
fáilte

My Christmas Rose,

I'll Give to you

Some Irish Loving

as gentle, soft as your bosom
as strong, passionate as the
Tempest
as close, united
for eternity
as only your husband
can love you

SHJ 81

See the poem on p. 129

Edna O'Brien

Some Irish Loving

A SELECTION

HARPER & ROW, PUBLISHERS
NEW YORK

Cambridge
Hagerstown
Philadelphia
San Francisco

London
Mexico City
São Paulo
Sydney

1817

FIRST U.S. EDITION

ISBN: 0-06-013192-6

LIBRARY OF CONGRESS CATALOG CARD NUMBER: 78-20180

79 80 81 82 83 84 10 9 8 7 6 5 4 3 2 1

I HAVE DELIBERATELY called this *Some Irish Loving*
because of course there is much that I have omitted. Some
of the omission is due to the sin of neglect and some to
a desire to omit the more reverent and the more
customary passages that have been used again and again.
Matthew Arnold is said to have thought Keats's letters to
Fanny Brawne ill-bred. I can think of no better adjective
to depict a state that has little to do with breeding and
much to do with the transportation of body and soul.

I would like to dedicate the book to those Irish men
and women who have been brave enough to fall in love
and foolish enough to commit it to paper. But if I am
allowed a favourite I would like to dedicate it to J. M.
Synge for his letters to Maire O'Neill because these to me
are the last word in truth, in beauty and in love.

No pleasure is risk-free.

Goethe

Love is a sickness and a smart
'Tis idly spoken
He will not give me back my heart
For it is broken.

Irishmen and Irishwomen regard sex
instinctively as they regard mud.

Arland Ussher

Contents

The Preamble

DEPENDING ON ONE'S SEX and one's religious propensities, love can be a skiff of magic power or a simple gaze on God. But not for the Irish, for whom everything is more copious, more trenchant and in the Domesday Book probably more consequential.

The very definition of love in the Irish dictionary lists branches of that 'malady' that may come as a surprise. Apart from love being love, affection, charity, interest, it is also unshared affection, a love of one in absence, a love of the unseen and a love of the little jug which of course is a drink. Battle and strife have a higher place in the ancient annals and it would be easier to tackle a theme that concerned The Adventures of Black Tadgh, The Visions of Saint Fursa or The Battle of the Red Fort. The more righteous would have us believe that the Irish kept those lubbard appetites concerning love and passion in due subordination. But if that were so, the race would have vanished. Despite prognostications about the Vanishing Irish and about the excess of bachelors, the country is still there and in it people busily engaged in the drama of love.

What is love?

> Of Heaven 'tis the brightest amazement,
> The blackest abasement of Hell,

A struggle for breath with a spectre,
    In nectar a choking to death;
'Tis a race with Heaven's lightning and thunder,
    Then Champion Feats under Moyle's water;
'Tis pursuing the cuckoo, the wooing
    Of Echo, the Rock's airy daughter.

What is Love?
Early Irish

It is savagery in the blood, and pain in the bone, and greed and despair in the mind. It is to be thirsty in the night and unslaked in the day. It is to carry memory like a thorn in the heart. It is to drip one's blood as one walks.

From *Deirdre*
by James Stephens

Love is a treachery of the flesh.
School-girl

The Fantastic

THE HEROES OF ANCIENT IRELAND had commitments such
as did not allow mere love or carnal passion to take
precedence. Valour, strength and chivalry were the first
requirements of a knight who had to plight his troth to his
tribe, by putting himself in dire predicaments long before he
chose a bride and her bondswomen. In fact having done
these things one wonders how he had time at his disposal for
the wooing and the cavort. Mercifully he was saved (and so
was she) the dreary drudge of everyday life, caught up as he
was with warfare, chess playing and the sylvan slaughter.

As a test of endurance he was planted in a pit or trench
that reached to his knees, armed with shield and a hazel staff
so as to face nine warriors with nine javelins who cast these
weapons about him. If he chanced to receive a single wound
he was not admitted to the order of the brave. Furthermore,
his hair having been plaited, he had to run through a thick
wood, with but the odds of a single tree placed between him
and his pursuers and if they came upon him and wounded
him he had also failed. Nor was it possible that his weapons
should tremble in his hands. Nor a single braid of his hair to
be loosened out of its plait and caught in a branch as he ran.

7

No, nor a single branch broken under his foot. And he must jump a tree as high as his forehead and stoop under one as low as his knee. And he must be able to pluck a thorn out of his heel with his hand, without stopping course. No doubt these fortified him as a man and as a lover. The intimacy with the woman is usually glossed over or smothered in decorous words. For instance, when Niamh the daughter of Angus, King of Munster, eloped with Ossian we learn that he was with her for six weeks, enjoying the hunting and venery of Ulida, and that the damsel with her thirty bondswomen used to come each morning and, in the blue-surfaced water of the lake, wash their hands and faces. Her father's warriors come in pursuit of her and as she sees them she cries out 'Alas for it!' and is happy to die, to be slain for her love. She laid her face to the ground, along with her thirty women companions, and a lump of black blood passed from her mouth which was considered to be her heart. Not all women died so nobly; some, being villainous, wrought death on the men who came to them in the green and grassy places.

> Lightly they lay and pleasured
> In the green grass of that guileless place
> Ladhra was the first to die;
> He perished of an embrace.
>
> Bith was buried in a stone heap,
> Riot of mind, all passion spent.
> Fintan fled from the ferocious women
> Lest he, too, by love be rent.

> From *The Book of Invasions*
> by R. A. S. MacAllister

Cuchulain, a mythological hero, was beautiful in form, could fight singly with the might of a horde and possessed such an inner heat that the snow melted around him. Forever a warrior, blood on his spear, blood on his sword, his white body black with blood, his soft skin furrowed with sword-cuts, wounds on his thighs and his eyes red as flame. He was so deft with a sword that he could cut a man in half and the one half of him would not miss the other for some time after. He was not so lucky with women. He loved women, but was made mad by one and given blood to drink by his own mother, blood that presaged his death.

The courtship of his future wife, Emer, commenced in an orchard, a place as close to Paradise as one can imagine it. Their banter has all the tantalization of ritual and the hidden meaning of love. He finds her in a field, her companions all about her, engaged in the doing of needlework and fine embroidery. He perceives that she has the six gifts – the gift of beauty, the gift of voice, the gift of sweet speech, the gift of needlework, the gift of wisdom and the gift of chastity.

'Where are you come from?' she asked him. And he answered her in riddles so that her companions might not understand him.

'From Intide Emma.'

'Where did you sleep?'

'We slept in the house of the man that tends the cattle of the plain of Tethra.'

'What was your food there?'

'The ruin of a chariot was cooked for us.'

'Which way did you come?'

'Between the two mountains of the wood.'

'Which way did you take after that?'

'That is not hard to tell. From the cover of the Sea, over the Great Secret of the Túatha de Danaan, and the Foam of the horses of Emain, over the Morrigu's Garden, and the Great Sow's back; over the Marrow of the Woman, between the Boar and his Dam; over the Washing-place of the horses of Dea; between the King of Ana and his servant, to Mandchuile of the Four Corners of the World; over Great Crime and the Remnants of the Great Feast; between the Vat and the Little Vat, to the Gardens of Lugh, to the daughters of Tethra, the nephew of the King of the Fomor.'

'And what account have you to give of yourself?' said Emer.

'I am the nephew of the man that disappears in another in the wood of Badb,' said Cuchulain.

'And now, maiden,' he said, 'what account have you to give of yourself?'

'That is not hard to tell,' said Emer, 'but Teamhair upon the hills, a watcher that sees no one, an eel hiding in the water, a rush out of reach, a flame of hospitality and a road that cannot be entered.'

She tells him that he has not reached the summit of his heroism. Bristling under the imputation that her father's chariot chiefs and heroes are stronger, he takes an oath that his doings will be spoken of among the doings of the great heroes of the world.

He sails to Scotland to master the skills and feats of a warrior. It is a strange road, and for much of the time he is sad and downhearted, and sometimes he goes astray in his mind. Beasts and monsters rise before him. A young woman Uacthach, casts her eye upon him and at once the colour in her face begins to change so that she is white as a flower and then crimson, and in her needlework she puts the gold thread where silver should be and the silver where the gold should be. To defend her he has to fight Aoife, queen of the tribes and the greatest woman warrior in the world because of being versed in enchantments and witchcraft. When they attack one another she breaks his spear in pieces and his sword at the hilt. He thwarts her and then takes hold of her and lifts her on his shoulders and brings her down to where the army is, lays her upon the ground and holds his sword to her breast until she begs for life. He grants it to her. They give each other love and out of it a great sorrow comes long afterwards. The child she bears him, Conlaoch, meets him in combat and is unwittingly killed by his own father.

Versed now in war, chicanery and manly loving, Cuchulain returns to Emer's palace, and leaps with his hero's leap over three walls and, once within, attacks with such wizard power that men fall on all sides. He reaches Emer and her foster sisters and carries them out to the white fields where he gives such angry blows to his enemies that streams of blood darken it on every side.

His slaughtering done, he took Emer for wife and brought her home to the palace where the walls were of red yew with copper rivets, where the gold ornamental birds had shining carbuncles set in their heads and where a rod with silver apples could be struck to induce an overwhelming silence. Emer is the nut of his heart. He is so beautiful that the women of Ulster are blind from looking at his dazzle. But it is in the Book of Fate that he will fall in love with yet another.

One day some birds fly about and the women ask him to use his sling and catch them. All the women receive birds except for Emer and so vexed is she that she insists he go out and get her two more. The two birds who next come have a touch of the supernatural as they are chained together with a chain of red gold and are singing music that could lull a gathering. There is enchantment behind them. He puts a stone in his sling, makes a cast and misses.

'My grief,' he says and takes another stone, and makes another cast, and misses, and re-misses so that rage induces him to take his heavy spear and as it goes through one of the birds they dive down under the water. Vexation is on him and he lies against a rock and falls asleep. Two women in green cloaks come towards him. They smile at him, they stroke him with their wands and after they have gone he stands up in his sleep and asks his men to bring him not to the house of Emer but to the speckled house where he can sleep. And for a year he does not speak to any person. One of the women in green reappears and asks him to come with her. She wants his love for her sister Fand, a lady of the sea, whose love has fallen upon him. Regardless of his own will he has been struck by the sidhe. Emer is incensed, and questions why the brave men of Ulster cannot help her husband, cannot cure him of this folly. She begs him to think of heroism, of battle spoils, of the women who wait on him, of his body, beloved by her, smooth like crystal. But again the green lady asks him to come to Fand.

'I will not come on a woman's asking,' he says. He sends Lêag instead, and arriving on a copper ship to that island Lêag finds himself in a fairy place. The tall trees are of pure crimson with lasting flowers and every different kind of fruit is ripe at the same time. Fand is so beautiful that her name means a tear, a tear for her purity, for a transparent light that passes over the fire of her eyes. There was nothing in life with which she could be compared. She asks why Cuchulain does not come and Lêag says that he would not come on a woman's asking. Fand then summons him with the promise of the inimitable battle. And Cuchulian hearing that challenge and the description of the woman who could take wits from whole armies, rose, passed his hand over his face and felt a strengthening coming back to his mind. Fand saw him coming, his red blade lately blooded, dimples on his cheeks, a blaze from his eyeballs, his eyelashes black as beetles, and with woman's fatality says, 'We compelled him from afar.'

> From Murthemne he comes, we greet him,
> Young Cuchulain, the champion strong;
> We, compelled from afar to meet him,
> Daughters all of Aed Abra, throng.

The green-cloaked woman bids him hail and begs him to recount the deeds he has done. He talks of the great host that closed on him, the foes from under the sea, the three thousand that he fought, and the groan of the unearthly one as he neared his end. She chants his prowess:

> Hail to Cuchulain
> Mind undismayed
> Hero-like glorious
> Heart great and still
> Battle victorious
> Firm rock of skill.

He sleeps with the Lady Fand and he abides with her for a

month and at the end of the month he bids her farewell. But she is not ready to relinquish him.

'Tell me,' said Fand, 'to what place I may go for our tryst and I will be there.'

They made tryst at the strand that is known as the Yew Tree's Head. Now Emer is brought word of this, and on the day when Cuchulain and Lêag are engaged in chess play and Fand is sitting watching, Emer advances with an army of women, their knives whetted to slay. Cuchulain recites:

> Lêag! Look behind thee!
> Close to thine ear
> Wise, well-ranked women
> Press on us near;
> Bright on each bosom
> Shines the gold clasp;
> Knives, with green edges
> Whetted, they grasp.
> As for the slaughter
> Chariot chiefs race,
> Come Forgall's daughter;
> Changed is her face.

Cuchulain tells Fand to have no fear, that he will guard her from Emer and the raging women, and he approaches his wife and asks why should he forfeit the company of a woman who is fair, bright, pure, well skilled, a fit mate for a monarch, one who can ride the billows of the ocean, one who is lovely in countenance, lofty in race, one who owns steeds and cattle. Emer insists that the lady to whom he clings is no better than she herself. She reminds him that everything new is fair, but that everything well known is sour, that men worship what they lack and that what they have seems paltry. She appeals to his memory and says how once they dwelt together, how they could do so again if only she could find favour in his sight! As she grieves, a fellow grief comes upon him and Fand realizes that she must surrender him.

'Desert me then,' cries Fand.

'Nay,' said Emer, 'it is more fitting that I should be the deserted one.'

But Fand knew that she had lost him and dissertates on her own fate:

> Emer! noble lady!
> Take thy man to thee:
> Though my arms resign him,
> Longing lives in me,
> Mighty need compels me,
> I must go on my way.
> Fame for other waiteth,
> Would I here could stay.

Betrayed, she goes back to the sea, and Cuchulain realizing his dilemma, bounded three times into the air until he came to a place of rushes where he abode for a long time, having no meat and no drink, dwelling in the mountains alone. Emer sent enchanters that they might bind him fast and bring him home, and though he strove against them they managed to hold him down and fed him a drink that was a drink of forgetfulness so that he would not remember Fand again, and they gave Emer a drink so that she might forget her jealousy; and the sea god shook his cloak between Cuchulain and Fand so that they might never meet again throughout all eternity.

His eventual death merited as much passion and verbal splendour as did his vicarious life. Emer beheld his lopped head and his lopped hand and lamented him. She bade Conall to make a wide very deep grave and she laid herself down beside her gentle comrade, and she put her mouth to his mouth and she said:

'Love of my life, my friend, my sweetheart, my one choice of the men of the earth, many is the woman, wed or unwed, envied me until today, and now I will not stay living after you.'

The last word however leaves room for ambiguity. All the living queens that loved Cuchulain saw him re-appear in his chariot and could hear him singing to them. Perhaps

Emer's death was precipitate?

To ask an Irish person what he or she means by love is to lay oneself open to very diverse and heated answers. On a random query I was amazed and bombarded, receiving answers ranging from the devout to the incredulous. Love, I was told, was sitting opposite a boy in front of a fire in Galway and flinging hot coals from the end of a tongs on to his feet. Love in Monaghan was any attempt to push a girl off a bicycle. Love in the backward parts of Galway and Mayo was for a young girl to marry an old bachelor and be expected to sleep with his bachelor brothers. Love was a pact with Satan invoked after dark by throwing thread into a lime kiln and calling on him to wield his lustful powers. Love was exclusive: 'Your face turned to mine and your head turned away from all others.' Love was a man performing his skills naked at the request of a woman and very often being speared for it. Love was crouching on one's hunkers with a hand under each kneecap and hopping about the room followed by a gentleman in the same position, followed by further women and further men all crouching until they sprawled onto the floor in a mass orgy. Love was an affectionate husband who put his wife's shoes inside her coffin. Love was forcing one's glass into the apparently reluctant lips of a young girl.

> I would coax her on my knee
> And sure I would go awhile
> Beneath the corner of her mantle.

In the heroic romances the woman was often a nymph of modesty and learning, the love knew no blight, as with the aid of the supernatural, every obstacle was overcome, even that demon known as jealousy.

From THE COURTSHIP OF ETAIN
translated by A. H. Leahy

And her name was Etain the daughter of Etar, who was the
king of Echrad. And his messengers returned to Eochaid, and
they told him of the maiden, of her form, and her grace, and
her countenance. And Eochaid came to that place to take the
maiden thence, and this was the way that he took; for as he
crossed over the ground where men hold the assembly of Bri
Leith, he saw the maiden at the brink of the spring. A clear
comb of silver was held in her hand, the comb was adorned
with gold; and near her, as for washing, was a bason of silver
whereon four birds had been chased, and there were little
bright gems of carbuncle on the rims of the bason. A bright
purple mantle waved round her; and beneath it was another
mantle, ornamented with silver fringes: the outer mantle was
clasped over her bosom with a golden brooch. A tunic she
wore, with a long hood that might cover her head attached to
it; it was stiff and glossy with green silk beneath red embroidery of gold, and was clasped over her breasts with marvell-
ously wrought clasps of silver and gold; so that men saw the
bright gold and the green silk flashing against the sun. On
her head were two tresses of golden hair, and each tress had
been plaited into four strands; at the end of each strand was
a little ball of gold. And there was that maiden, undoing her
hair that she might wash it, her two arms out through the
armholes of her smock. Each of her two arms was as white
as the snow of a single night, and each of her cheeks was as
rosy as the foxglove. Even and small were the teeth in her
head, and they shone like pearls. Her eyes were as blue as
a hyacinth, her lips delicate and crimson; very high, soft and
white were her shoulders. Tender, polished, and white were
her wrists; her fingers long, and of great whiteness; her nails
were beautiful and pink. White as the snow, or as the foam
of the wave, was her side; long was it, slender and as soft
as silk. Smooth and white were her thighs; her knees were
round and firm and white; her ankles were as straight as the

rule of a carpenter. Her feet were slim, and as white as the ocean's foam; evenly set were her eyes; her eyebrows were of a bluish black, such as ye see upon the shell of a beetle. Never a maid fairer than she, or more worthy of love, was till then seen by the eyes of men; and it seemed to them that she must be one of those who have come from the fairy mounds: it is of this maiden that men have spoken when it hath been said: 'All that's graceful must be tested by Etain; all that's lovely by the standard of Etain.'

> Grace with Etain's grace compare!
> Etain's face shall test what's fair!

And desire of her seized upon the king; and he sent a man of his people in front of him to go to her kindred, in order that she might abide to await his coming. And afterwards the king came to the maiden, and he sought speech from her: 'Whence art thou sprung, O maiden?' says Eochaid, 'and whence is it that thou has come?' 'It is easy to answer thee,' said the maiden: 'Etain is my name, the daughter of the king of Echrad; "out of the fairy mound" am I.' 'Shall an hour of dalliance with thee be granted to me?' said Eochaid. ' 'Tis for that I have come hither under thy safeguard,' said she. 'And indeed twenty years have I lived in this place, ever since I was born in the mound where the fairies dwell; and the men who dwell in the elf-mounds, their kings and their nobles, have been a-wooing me: yet to never a one of them was granted sleep with me, for I have loved thee, and have set my love and affection upon thee; and that ever since I was a little child, and had first the gift of speech. It was for the high tales of thee, and of thy splendour, that I have loved thee thus; and though I have never seen thee before, I knew thee at once by reason of the report of thee that I had heard; it is thou, I know, to whom we have attained.' 'It is no evil-minded lover who now inviteth thee,' said Eochaid. 'Thou shalt be welcomed by me, and I will leave all women for thy sake and thine alone will I be so long as it is pleasing to thee.' 'Let the bride-price that befits me be paid,' said the maiden, 'and after that let my desire be fulfilled.' 'It shall be as thou hast said,' the king answered her; and he gave the value of seven cumals to be her bride-price; and after that he brought her to Tara, whereon a fair and hearty welcome was made to her.

Now there were three brothers of the one blood all sons of Finn, namely, Eochaid Airem, and Eochaid, and Ailill Anglonnach, or Ailill of the Single Stain, because the only stain that was upon him was the love that he had for his brother's wife. And at that time came all the men of Ireland to hold the festival of Tara; they were there for fourteen days before Samhain, the day when the summer endeth, and for fourteen days after that day. It was at the feast of Tara that love for Etain the daughter of Etar came upon Ailill Anglonnach; and ever so long as they were at the Tara Feast, so long he gazed upon the maid. And it was there that the wife of Ailill spoke to him; she who was the daughter of Luchta of the Red Hand, who came from the province of Leinster: 'Ailill,' said she, 'why dost thou gaze at her from afar? for long gazing is a token of love.' And Ailill gave blame to himself for this thing, and after that he looked not upon the maid.

Now it followed that after that the Feast of Tara had been consumed, the men of Ireland parted from one another, and then it was that Ailill became filled with the pangs of envy and of desire; and he brought upon himself the choking misery of a sore sickness, and was borne to the stronghold of Frémain in Tethba after that he had fallen into that woe. There also, until a whole year had ended, sickness long brooded over Ailill, and for long was he in distress, yet he allowed none to know of his sickness. And there Eochaid came to learn of his brother's state, and he came near to his brother, and laid his hand upon his chest; and Ailill heaved a sigh. 'Why,' said Eochaid, 'surely this sickness of thine is not such as to cause thee to lament; how fares it with thee?' 'By my word,' said Ailill, ' 'tis no easier that I grow; but it is worse each day, and each night.' 'Why, what ails thee?' said Eochaid, 'By my word of truth,' said Ailill, 'I know not.'

'Bring one of my folk hither,' said Eochaid, 'one who can find out the cause of this illness.'

Then Fachtna, the chief physician of Eochaid, was summoned to give aid to Ailill, and he laid his hand upon his chest, and Ailill heaved a sigh. 'Ah,' said Fachtna, 'there is no need for lament in this matter, for I know the cause of thy sickness; one or other of these two evils oppresseth thee, the pangs of envy, or the pangs of love; nor hast thou been aided to escape from them until now.' And Ailill was full of shame, and he refused to confess to Fachtna the cause of his illness, and the physician left him.

Now, after all this, king Eochaid went in person to make a royal progress throughout the realm of Ireland, and he left Etain behind him in his fortress; and 'Lady,' said he, 'deal thou gently with Ailill so long as he is yet alive; and, should he die,' said he, 'do thou see that his burial mound be heaped for him; and that a standing-stone be set up in memory of him; and let his name be written upon it in letters of Ogham.' Then the king went away for the space of a year, to make his royal progress throughout the realm of Ireland, and Ailill was left behind, in the stronghold of Frémain of Tethba; there to pass away and to die.

Now upon a certain day that followed, the lady Etain came to the house where Ailill lay in his sickness, and thus she spoke to him: 'What is it,' she said, 'that ails thee? thy sickness is great, and if we but knew anything that would content thee, thou shouldest have it.' It was thus that at that time she spoke, and she sang a verse of a song, and Ailill in song made answer to her:

Etain

Young man, of the strong step and splendid,
    What hath bound thee? what ill dost thou bear?
Thou hast long been on sick-bed extended,
    Though around thee the sunshine was fair.

19

Ailill

There is reason indeed for my sighing,
    I joy naught at my harp's pleasant sound;
Milk untasted beside me is lying;
    And by this in disease am I bound.

Etain

Tell me all, thou poor man, of thine ailing;
    For a maiden am I that is wise;
Is there naught, that to heal thee availing,
    Thou couldst win by mine aid, and arise?

Ailill

If I told thee, thou beautiful maiden,
    My words, as I formed them, would choke,
For with fire can eyes' curtains be laden:
    Woman-secrets are evil, if woke.

Etain

It is ill woman-secrets to waken;
    Yet with Love, its remembrance is long;
And its part by itself may be taken,
    Nor a thought shall remain of the wrong.

Ailill

I adore thee, white lady, as grateful;
    Yet thy bounty deserve I but ill:
To my soul is my longing but hateful,
    For my body doth strive with me still.

Eocho Fedlech, his bride to him taking,
    Made thee queen; and from thence is my woe:
For my head and my body are aching,
    And all Ireland my weakness must know.

If, among the white women who near me abide,
  There is one who is vexing, whose love thou dost hide:
To thy side will I bring her, if thus I may please:
  And in love thou shalt win her, thy sickness to ease.

'Ah lady!' said Ailill, 'easily could the cure of my sickness be wrought by the aid of thee, and great gain should there come from the deed, but thus it is with me until that be accomplished:

> 'Long ago did my passion begin,
>   A full year it exceeds in its length;
> And it holds me, more near than my skin,
>   And it rules over wrath in its strength.

> 'And the earth into four it can shake,
>   Can reach up to the heights of the sky;
> And a neck with its might it can break,
>   Nor from fight with a spectre would fly.

> 'In vain race up to heaven 'tis urged;
>   It is chilled, as with water, and drowned:
> 'Tis a weapon, in ocean submerged;
>   'Tis a desire for an echo, a sound.

> ' 'Tis thus my love, my passion seem;
>   'Tis thus I strive in vain
> To win the heart of her whose love
>   I long so much to gain.'

Now each day the lady came to Ailill to tend him, and to divide for him the portion of food that was allotted to him; and she wrought a great healing upon him: for it grieved her that he should perish for her sake. And one day the lady spoke to Ailill: 'Come thou to-morrow,' said she, 'to tryst with me at the break of day, in the house which lieth outside, and is beyond the fort, and there shalt thou have granted thy request and thy desire.' On that night Ailill lay without sleep until the coming of the morning; and when the time had come that was appointed for his tryst, his sleep lay heavily upon him; so that till the hour of his rise he lay deep in his sleep. And Etain went to the tryst, nor had she long to wait ere she saw a man coming towards her in the likeness of Ailill, weary and feeble; but she knew that he was not Ailill and she continued there waiting for Ailill. And the lady came back from her tryst, and Ailill awoke, and thought that he would rather die than live; and he went in great sadness and grief. And the lady came to speak with him, and when he told her what had befallen him: 'Thou shalt come,' said she, 'to the same place, to meet with me upon the morrow.' And upon the morrow it was the same as upon the first day; each day came that man to her tryst. And she came again upon the last day that was appointed for the tryst, and the same man met her. ' 'Tis not with thee that I trysted,' said she, 'why dost thou come to meet me? and for him whom I would have met here; neither from desire of his love nor for fear of danger from him had I appointed to meet him, but only to heal him, and to cure him from the sickness which had come upon him for his love of me.' 'It were more fitting for thee to come to tryst with me,' says the man, 'for when thou wast Etain of the Horses, and when thou wast the daughter of Ailill, I myself was thy husband.' 'Why,' said she, 'what name hast thou in the land? that is what I would demand of thee.' 'It is not hard to answer thee,' he said; 'Mider of Bri Leith is my name.' 'And what made thee to part from me, if we were as thou sayest?' said Etain. 'Easy again is the answer,' said Mider; 'it was the sorcery of Fuamnach and the spells of Bressal Etarlam that put us apart.' And Mider said to Etain: 'Wilt thou come with me?'

'Nay,' answered Etain, 'I will not exchange the king of all Ireland for thee; for a man whose kindred and whose lineage is unknown.' 'It was I myself indeed,' said Mider, 'who filled all the mind of Ailill with love for thee; it was

I also who prevented his coming to the tryst with thee, and allowed him not thine honour to spoil it.'

After all this the lady went back to her house and she came to speech with Ailill, and she greeted him. 'It hath happened well for us both,' said Ailill, 'that the man met thee there: for I am cured for ever from my illness, thou also art unhurt in thine honour, and may a blessing rest upon thee!' 'Thanks be to our gods,' said Etain, 'that both of us do indeed deem that all this hath chanced so well.' And after that Eochaid came back from his royal progress, and he asked at once for his brother; and the tale was told to him from the beginning to the end, and the king was grateful to Etain, in that she had been gracious to Ailill; and, 'What hath been related to this tale,' said Eochaid, 'is well-pleasing to ourselves.'

Jealousy has always been the whetstone of love and some would say that without it Love does not have its inner shiver. Mr J.M. Synge was told this story in Wicklow and it is how one man dealt with his wife's deceit.

HE THAT'S DEAD CAN DO NO HURT
by J. M. Synge

One day I was travelling on foot from Galway to Dublin, and the darkness came on me and I ten miles from the town I was wanting to pass the night in. Then a hard rain began to fall and I was tired walking, so when I saw a sort of a house with no roof on it up against the road, I got in the way the walls would give me shelter.

As I was looking round I saw a light in some trees two perches off, and thinking any sort of a house would be better than where I was, I got over a wall and went up to the house to look in at the window.

I saw a dead man laid on a table, and candles lighted, and a woman watching him. I was frightened when I saw him, but it was raining hard, and I said to myself, if he was dead he couldn't hurt me. Then I knocked on the door and the woman came and opened it.

'Good evening, ma'am,' says I.

'Good evening kindly, stranger,' says she. 'Come in out of the rain.'

Then she took me in and told me her husband was after dying on her, and she was watching him that night.

'But it's thirsty you'll be, stranger,' says she. 'Come into the parlour.'

Then she took me into the parlour – and it was a fine clean house – and she put a cup, with a saucer under it, on the table before me with fine sugar and bread.

When I'd had a cup of tea, I went back into the kitchen where the dead man was lying, and she gave me a fine new pipe off the table with a drop of spirits.

'Stranger,' says she, 'would you be afeared to be alone with himself?'

'Not a bit in the world, ma'am,' says I; 'he that's dead can do no hurt.'

Then she said she wanted to go over and tell the neighbours the way her husband was after dying on her, and she went out and locked the door behind her.

I smoked one pipe, and I leaned out and took another off the table. I was smoking it with my hand on the back of my chair – the way you are yourself this minute, God bless you – and I looking on the dead man, when he opened his eyes as wide as myself and looked at me.

'Don't be afraid, stranger,' said the dead man; 'I'm not

24

dead at all in the world. Come here and help me up and I'll tell you all about it.'

Well, I went up and took the sheet off of him, and I saw that he had a fine clean shirt on his body, and fine flannel drawers.

He sat up then, and says he –

'I've got a bad wife, stranger, and I let on to be dead the way I'd catch her goings on.'

Then he got two fine sticks he had to keep down his wife, and he put them at each side of his body, and he laid himself out again as if he was dead.

In half an hour his wife came back and a young man along with her. Well, she gave him his tea, and she told him he was tired, and he would do right to go and lie down in the bedroom.

The young man went in and the woman sat down to watch by the dead man. A while after she got up and 'Stranger,' says she, 'I'm going in to get the candle out of the room; I'm thinking the young man will be asleep by this time.' She went into the bedroom, but the divil a bit of her came back.

Then the dead man got up, and he took one stick, and he gave the other to myself. We went in and saw them lying together with her head on his arm.

The dead man hit him a blow with the stick so that the blood out of him leapt up and hit the gallery.

That is my story.

A LEARNED MISTRESS
translated by Frank O'Connor

Tell him it's all a lie;
I love him as much as my life;
He needn't be jealous of me –
I love him and loathe his wife.

If he kill me through jealousy now
His wife will perish of spite,
He'll die of grief for his wife –
Three of us dead in a night.

All blessings from heaven to earth
On the head of the woman I hate,
And the man I love as my life,
Sudden death be his fate.

The jealousy and the singular possessiveness may be true for some but it is not so for Mr Samuel Beckett who even debates on the name of his love object and wonders if she is not one and the same person as his own mother. He knows with a seer's grim knowledge that all things run in together in the body's long madness.

From MOLLOY
by Samuel Beckett

I have rubbed up against a few men in my time, but women? Oh well, I may as well confess it now, yes, I once rubbed up against one. I don't mean my mother, I did more than rub up against her. And if you don't mind we'll leave my mother out of all this. But another who might have been my mother, and even I think my grandmother, if chance had not willed otherwise. Listen to him now talking about chance. It was she made me acquainted with love. She went by the peaceful name of Ruth I think, but I can't say for certain. Perhaps the name was Edith. She had a hole between her legs, oh not the bunghole I had always imagined, but a slit, and in this I put, or rather she put, my so-called virile member, not without difficulty, and I toiled and moiled until I discharged or gave up trying or was begged by her to stop. A mug's game in my opinion and tiring on top of that, in the long run. But I lent myself to it with a good enough grace, knowing it was love, for she had told me so. She bent over the couch, because of her rheumatism, and in I went from behind. It was the only position she could bear, because of her lumbago. It seemed all right to me, for I had seen dogs, and I was astonished when she confided that you could go about it differently. I wonder what she meant exactly. Perhaps after all she put me in her rectum. A matter of complete indifference to me, I needn't tell you. But is it true love, in the rectum? That's what bothers me sometimes. Have I never known true love, after all? She too was an eminently flat woman and she moved with short stiff steps, leaning on an ebony stick. Perhaps she too was a man, yet another of them. But in that case surely our testicles would have collided, while we writhed. Perhaps she held hers tight in her hand, on purpose to avoid it. She favoured voluminous tempestuous shifts and petticoats and other undergarments whose names I forget. They welled up all frothing and swishing and then, congress achieved, broke over us in slow cascades. And all I could see was her taut yellow nape which every now and then I set my teeth in, forgetting I had none, such is the power of instinct. We met in a rubbish dump, unlike any other, and yet they are all alike, rubbish dumps. I don't know what she was doing there. I was limply poking about in the garbage saying probably, for at that age I must still have been capable of general ideas. This is life. She had no time to lose, I had nothing to lose, I would have made love with a goat, to know what love was. She had a dainty flat, no, not dainty, it made you want to lie down in a corner and never get up again. I liked it. It was full of dainty furniture, under our desperate strokes the couch moved forward on its castors, the whole place fell about our ears, it was pandemonium. Our commerce was not without tenderness, with trembling hands she cut my toe-nails and I rubbed her rump with winter cream. This idyll was of short duration. Poor Edith, I hastened her end perhaps. Anyway it was she who started it, in the rubbish dump, when she laid her hand upon my fly. More precisely, I was bent double over a heap of muck, in the hope of finding something to disgust me for ever with eating, when she, undertaking me from behind, thrust her stick between my legs and began to titillate my privates. She gave me money after each session, to me who would have consented to know love, and probe it to the bottom, without charge. But she was an idealist. I would have preferred it seems to me an orifice less arid and roomy, that would have given me a higher opinion of love it seems to me. However. 'Twixt finger and thumb 'tis heaven in comparison. But love is no doubt above such base contingencies. And not when you are comfortable, but when your frantic member casts about for a rubbing-place, and the unction of a little mucous membrane, and meeting with none does not beat in retreat, but retains its tumefaction, it is then no doubt that true love comes to pass, and wings away, high above the tight fit and the loose. And when you add a little pedicure and massage, having nothing to do with the instant of bliss strictly speaking, then I feel no further doubt is justified, in this connection. The other thing that bothers me, in this connection, is the indifference with which I learnt of her death, one black night I was crawling towards her, an indifference softened indeed by the pain of losing a source of revenue. She died taking a warm tub, as her custom was before receiving me. It limbered her up. When I think she might have expired in my arms! The tub overturned and the dirty water spilt all over the floor and down on top of the lodger below, who gave the alarm. Well, well, I didn't think I knew this story so well. She must have been a woman after all, if she hadn't been it would have got around in the neighbourhood. It is true they were extraordi-

28

narily reserved, in my part of the world, about everything connected with sexual matters. But things have perhaps changed since my time. And it is quite possible that the fact of having found a man when they should have found a woman was immediately repressed and forgotten, by the few unfortunate enough to know about it. And it is quite possible that everybody knew about it, and spoke about it, with the sole exception of myself. But there is one thing that torments me, when I delve into all this, and that is to know whether all my life has been devoid of love or whether I really met with it, in Ruth. What I do know for certain is that I never sought to repeat the experience, having I suppose the intuition that it had been unique and perfect, of its kind, achieved and inimitable, and that it behoved me to preserve its memory, pure of all pastiche, in my heart, even if it meant my resorting from time to time to the alleged joys of so-called self-abuse.

The idea of the unromantic love, of love that is dark, unpretty, dour and even barbarous does not begin with Mr Beckett. This next tale, which is probably eighteenth century, was found in St Patrick's College, Maynooth, a seminary for training to the priesthood.

From THE ROMANCE OF MIS AND DUBH RUIS

translated by David Greene

Mis, the daughter of Dáire Dóidgheal, sang this, lamenting her mate and companion Dubh Ruis, the sweet harper of Feidhlim the son of Criomthann, the king of Munster. For the soldiers of Clanmaurice killed this Dubh Ruis when he went to levy on them the tribute that King Feidhlim had given him for subduing Mis the daughter of Dáire and restoring her to her senses. For she was a 'geilt' [lunatic] for seven score years (or according to others for three hundred years) on Slieve Mish in the barony of Clanmaurice, near Tralee in County Kerry, from the day her father Dáire the Great was killed, when he came to conquer Ireland in the battle of Ventry. For he brought her with him, since she was his only daughter, and, when the battle was over, she came with many others to look for her father's body amongst the slaughter, and when she found the body with its many wounds, she began to suck and drink the blood from the wounds, so that she flew away in the end in a fever of madness to Slieve Mish, and remained there for the aforesaid time, so that fur and hair grew on her, so long that it trailed on the ground behind. And the nails of her feet and hands grew so excessively that there was no beast or person she would meet but she would tear apart immediately.

And the flight of her madness gave her such a speed of movement that she would run like the wind and overtake in running anything she pleased, and there was no animal or person she killed but she would eat and drink whatever she wished of its flesh and blood, so that a desert stripped of people and cattle was created for fear of her in that part of the country which is called the barony of Clanmaurice, for King Feidhlim issued a general proclamation that she should not be killed for any reason. However, he offered and promised great rewards, together with the tributes of the same barony, to the man who would take or capture her alive.

Many journeyed to attempt her one after the other, so that the majority perished by her in the venture. However, Dubh Ruis, the harper, said at last to Feidhlim the king that he himself would attempt her with his harp; and the king laughed at him, but Dubh Ruis asked for a handful of gold and a handful of silver, which were necessary for the venture, to be given to him and he would go to attempt her. The king gave him the gold and the silver and he made no stay until he reached Slieve Mish. And when he reached the mountain, he sat down in the place where he thought she might be found, spread his cloak or mantle under him, and scattered the gold and the silver on the edges of the cloak. He lay on his back. He put the harp on his body. He opened his trousers or his breeches and bared himself, for he thought that if he could lie with her and know her, it would be a good means and device for bringing her to her sense or her natural reason. He was not long thus before she came to the spot, having heard the music, and she stood looking savagely at him and listening to the music.

'Aren't you a man?' said she. 'I am,' said he. 'What is this?' said she, putting her hand on the harp. 'A harp,' said he. 'Ho, ho!' said she, 'I remember the harp; my father had one like it. Play it for me.' 'I will,' said he, 'but don't do me any damage or harm.' 'I won't,' said she. Then she looked at the gold and silver and said, 'What are these?' 'Gold and silver,' said he. 'I remember,' said she, 'my father had gold. Och, ochone!'

As she looked at him, she caught sight of his nakedness and his members of pleasure. 'What are those?' she said, pointing to his bag or his eggs – and he told her. 'What is this?' said she, about the other thing that she saw. 'That is the wand of the feat,' said he. 'I do not remember that,' said she, 'my father hadn't anything like that. The wand of the feat; what is the feat?' 'Sit beside me,' said he, 'and I will do the feat of the wand for you.' 'I will,' said she, 'and stay you with me.' 'I will,' said he, and lay with her and knew her, and she said, 'Ha, ba, ba, that was a good feat; do it again.' 'I will,' said he; 'however, I will play the harp for you first.' 'Don't mind the harp,' said she, 'but do the feat.' 'I wish to partake of food,' said he, 'for I am hungry.' 'I will get you a stag,' said she. 'Do, and I have bread myself.' 'Where is it?' said she. 'Here it is,' said he. 'Ha, ha, I remember the bread; my father used to have it. Don't go away,' said she. 'I will not,' said he.

It was not long before she returned with a strangled stag under her arm, and she was going to tear it apart to eat it as it was, when Dubh Ruis said to her, 'Wait, and I will bleed the stag and cook the flesh.' Then he cut the stag's throat and skinned it. And he made a great fire of the forest brushwood and gathered a heap of granite stones and put them in the fire. He made a wide round hole in the ground and filled it with water. He cut up the meat and wrapped it in a bundle of sedge, and wrapped a straw rope round it, and put it into the hole, and kept feeding and sinking those thoroughly heated, red-hot stones into the water, and kept it boiling all the time until the meat was cooked. He took it out of the hole and put the fat of the stag into the boiling water so that it melted. Then he spread out on the stag's hide his meat and bread and told her to come and eat her meal, for she had been watching him peacefully and wonderingly all this time. 'I remember,' said she, 'that it is cooked meat my father used to have, and I know that it is best that way, and not the way I had it.' With that, Dubh Ruis broke the bread and carved the meat for her, and made her eat her fill quietly and contentedly, so that she said that she would do whatever he told her if only he would stay with her. Then he brought her fresh water in his cloak or his helmet, and she drank her fill of it.

Then he brought her to the hole in which the lukewarm broth and the melted fat of the stag was, and put her standing in it, and took the hide of the deer and rubbed and kneaded the joints of her body and her bones, and began to scrub and scour and polish her with the fat of the stag and with the broth, until he cleaned her a great deal and brought streams of sweat from her. He collected foliage and moss and green rushes and made a bed for her; he spread the hide of the stag under her and his cloak over her. He lay down beside her, and knew her, and so they slept till morning. However he could not waken her in the morning, so he arose and dressed himself and built a hut or shelter of the tops and branches of trees over her, and she did not wake till evening, and when she did not find him with her, she began to lament (and he was secretly listening to her) and to say, amongst other things:

> It is not the gold I weep for, the sweet
> > harp or the eggs,
> But the wand of the feat which Dubh Ruis,
> > son of Raghnall, had.

From THE POOR MOUTH
by Myles na Gopaleen

– Honest fellow! said I, I'm two years waiting now without a wife and I don't think I'll ever do any good without one. I'm afraid the neighbours are mocking me. Do you think is there any help for the fix I'm in or will I be all alone until the day of my death and everlasting burial?

– Bow! said the Old-Fellow, 'twould be necessary for you to know some girl.

– If that's the way, I replied, where do you think the best girls are to be got?

– In the Rosses, without a doubt!

The Sea-cat entered my mind and I became a little worried. However, there is little use denying the truth and I trusted the Old-Fellow.

– If 'tis that way, said I in a bold voice, I'll go to the Rosses tomorrow to get a woman.

The Old-Fellow was dissatisfied with this kind of thing and endeavoured for a while to coax me from the marriage-fever that had come upon me but, of course, I had no desire to break the resolution which was fixed for a year in my mind. He yielded finally and informed my mother of the news.

– Wisha! said she, the poor creature!

– If he manages to get a woman out of the Rosses, said the Old-Grey-Fellow, how do we know but that she'll have a dowry? Wouldn't the likes of that be a great help to us at present in this house when the spuds are nearly finished and the last drop reached in the end of the bottle with us?

– I wouldn't say that you haven't the truth of it! said my mother.

They decided at last to yield completely to me. The Old-Fellow said that he was acquainted with a man in Gweedore who had a nice curly-headed daughter who was, as yet, un-married although the young men from the two sandbanks were all about her, frenzied with eagerness to marry. Her father was named Jams O'Donnell and Mabel was the maiden's name. I said that I would be satisfied to accept her. The following day the Old-Fellow put a five-noggin bottle in his pocket and both of us set out in the direction of Gwee-dore. In the middle of the afternoon we reached that town-land after a good walk while the daylight was still in the heavens. Suddenly the Old-Fellow halted and sat down by the roadside.

– Are we yet near the habitation and enduring home of the gentleman, Jams O'Donnell? asked I softly and quietly, querying the Old-Fellow.

– We are! said he. There is his house over yonder.

– Fair enough, said I. Come on till we settle the deal and get our evening spuds. There's a sharp hunger on my hunger.

– Little son! said the Old-Fellow sorrowfully, I'm afraid that you don't understand the world. 'Tis said in the good books that describe the affairs of the Gaelic paupers that it's in the middle of the night that two men come visiting if they have a five-noggin bottle and are looking for a woman. Therefore we must sit here until the middle of the night comes.

– But 'twill be wet tonight. The skies above are full.

– Never mind! There's no use for us trying to escape from fate, oh bosom friend!

We did not succeed in escaping that night either from fate or the rain. We were drenched into the skin and to the bones. When we reached Jams O'Donnell's floor finally, we were completely saturated, water running from us freely, wetting both Jams and his house as well as every thing and living creature present. We quenched the fire and it had to be rekindled nine times.

Mabel was in bed (or had gone to her bed) but there is no necessity for me to describe the stupid conversation carried on by the Old-Fellow and Jams when they were discussing the question of the match. All the talk is available in the books which I have mentioned previously. When we left Jams at the bright dawn of day, the girl was betrothed to me and the Old-Fellow was drunk. We reached Corkadoragha at the midhour of day and were well satisfied with the night's business.

I need hardly remark that there were revelry and high frolics in this townland when my wedding-day came. The neighbours arrived to congratulate me. The Old-Fellow had, by this time, drunk the dowry-money which he had procured and there was not a good drop in the house to offer to the neighbours. When they realized that matters were thus, gloom and ill-humour took hold of them. Threatening whispers were heard from the men occasionally and the women set themselves to devouring all our potatoes and drinking all our butter-milk so as to inflict a three-months' scarcity upon us. A species of terror came upon the Old-Fellow when he saw how matters stood with the company. He whispered privily in my ear.

35

– Fellow! said he, if this gang doesn't get spirits and tobacco from us, I'm afraid one of our pigs will be stolen from us this night.

– All the pigs and my wife will be stolen as well, sir, I replied.

Mabel was in the end of the house at this juncture with my mother on top of her. The poor girl was trying to escape back to her father's house and my mother endeavouring to make her see reason and informing her that it is compulsory to submit to Gaelic fate. There was great weeping and tumult that night in our house.

It was Martin O'Bannassa himself who rescued us. When everything was truly in a bad state, he walked in carrying a small barrel of true water under his armpit. He quietly presented me with the barrel and congratulated me courteously on my marriage. When the company inside realized that the door of hospitality was finally opened, they wished to be merry and good-humoured and commenced to drink, dance and make music with all their might. After some time, they made a racket which shook the walls of the house, dismaying and terrorizing the pigs. The woman in the end of the house was given a full cup of that fiery water – despite the fact that she had no stomach for it – and before long she ceased her struggling and fell into a drunken slumber in the rushes. According as the men drank their fill, they lost the inherited good manners and good habits they had. By the time midnight had come, blood was being spilled liberally and there were a few men in the company without a stitch of clothing about them. At three in the morning, two men died after a bout of fighting which arose in the end of the house – poor Gaelic paupers without guile who had no experience of the lightning-water in Martin's barrel. As for the Old-Fellow, he almost faced eternity together with the other two. He was not in the fight and no blow was struck on him but during the dancing he sat in a place near the barrel. I considered that it was a good thing that my wife lost her senses and was not aware of the conduct of that wedding-feast. There was no sweet sound there and any hand which was raised did not accomplish a good deed.

Yes! when I had been married a month or so, contention and angry speech arose between my wife and my mother. The situation worsened daily and at last the Old-Fellow advised us to clear out of the house altogether and to settle down in another place because, said he, it has always been thus with every newly-wed couple. It was neither right nor proper, said he, that two women should live under the same roof. It was clear to me that the trouble between them was annoying him and disturbing his night's sleep. We adapted for our habitation the old hut which had been formerly built for the animals. When that was accomplished, and we had installed the beds of rushes, I and my wife left the other house together with two pigs and a few small household effects to begin life in the new domicile. Mabel was skilled in potato-boiling and we lived together peacefully for a year, both of us companionable in the end of the house. Often the Old-Grey-Fellow came in to converse with us in the afternoon.

Yes! life is extraordinary. One time when I returned from Galway in the black of night, what do you think I noticed but that we had acquired a new piglet in the end of the house. My wife was sleeping while the tiny little bright-skinned thing was squealing in the centre of the house. I took it care-fully and allowed it to drop from my hand with amazement when I realized precisely what I had. It had a small bald head, a face as large as a duck-egg and legs like my own. I had a baby-child. Need I say that the sudden raising of my heart was both joyous and indescribable? We had a young male child! I felt importance and superiority filling my heart and substance coming in my body!

I let the kitten gently down alongside his mother and rushed out to the Old-Fellow, holding a bottle of spirits which I had kept hidden for a year. We drank a glass and yet another glass together in the darkness and then we drank the health of the young son. After some time, when some of the neighbours heard the shouting and the inebriated commotion that we caused, they knew that true water was available for nothing and they arose from their rushy beds and congregated in to keep us company. We had a great night until morning. We decided to name the young man Leonardo O'Coonassa.

Alas! happiness is not lasting and neither is joy for any Gaelic pauper because he does not escape for long the scourging of fate. One day, while playing on the sward in front of the door with Leonardo when he was a year and a day old, I noticed some indisposition come suddenly upon him and that he was not far from eternity. His little face was grey and a destructive cough attacked his throat. I grew terrified when I could not calm the creature. I left him down on the grass and ran in to find my wife. What do you think but that I found her stretched out, cold in death on the rushes, her mouth wide open while the pigs snorted around her. When I reached Leonardo again in the place I had left him, he was also lifeless. He had returned whence he had come.

Here then, reader, is some evidence for you of the life of the Gaelic paupers in Corkadoragha and an account of the fate which awaits them from their first day. After great merriment comes sorrow and good weather never remains for ever.

From THE BROWN MAN
by Gerald Griffin

'Come in, wife; this is my palace,' said the bridegroom.

'What! a clay-hovel, worse than my mother's!' They dismounted, and the horse and the dog disappeared in an instant, with a horrible noise, which the girl did not know whether to call snorting, barking, or laughing.

'Are you hungry?' said the Brown Man. 'If so, there is your dinner.'

'A handful of raw white-eyes, and a grain of salt!'

'And when you are sleepy, here is your bed,' he continued, pointing to a little straw in a corner, at sight of which Nora's limbs shivered and trembled again. It may be easily supposed that she did not make a very hearty dinner that evening, nor did her husband neither.

In the dead of the night, when the clock of Mucruss Abbey had just tolled one, a low neighing at the door, and a soft barking at the window were heard. Nora feigned sleep. The Brown Man passed his hand over her eyes and face. She snored.

'I'm coming,' said he, and he arose gently from her side. In half an hour after she felt him by her side again. He was cold as ice.

The next night the same summons came. The Brown Man rose. The wife feigned sleep. He returned cold. The morning came.

The next night came. The bell tolled at Mucruss, and was heard across the lakes. The Brown Man rose again, and passed a light before the eyes of the feigning sleeper. None slumber so sound as they who *will* not wake. Her heart trembled, but her frame was quiet and firm. A voice at the door summoned the husband.

'You are very long coming. The earth is tossed up, and I am hungry. Hurry! Hurry! Hurry! if you would not lose all.'

'I'm coming!' said the Brown Man. Nora rose and followed instantly. She beheld him at a distance winding through a lane of frost-nipt sallow trees. He often paused and looked back, and once or twice retraced his steps to within a few yards of the tree behind which she had shrunk. The moonlight, putting the shadow close and dark about her, afforded the best concealment. He again proceeded, and she followed. In a few minutes they reached the old Abbey of Mucruss. With a sickening heart she saw him enter the churchyard. The wind rushed through the huge yew tree and startled her. She mustered courage enough, however, to reach the gate of the churchyard and look in. The Brown Man, the horse and the dog were there seated by an open grave, eating something, and glancing their brown, fiery eyes about in every direction. The moonlight shone full on them and her. Looking down towards her shadow on the earth, she started with horror to observe it move, although she was herself perfectly still. It waved its black arms and motioned her back. What the feasters said, she understood not, but she seemed still fixed in the spot. She looked once more on her shadow; it raised one hand, and pointed the way to the lane; then slowly rising from the ground, and confronting her, it walked rapidly off in that direction. She followed as quickly as might be.

She was scarcely in her straw, when the door creaked behind, and her husband entered. He lay down by her side and started.

'Uf! Uf!' said she, pretending to be just awakened, 'how cold you are, my love!'

'Cold, inagh? Indeed you are not very warm yourself, my dear, I'm thinking.'

'Little admiration I shouldn't be warm, and you leaving me alone this way at night, till my blood is snow broth, no less.'

'Umph!' said the Brown Man, as he passed his arm round her waist. 'Ha! your heart is beating fast?'

'Little admiration it should. I am not well, indeed. Them praties and salt don't agree with me at all.'

'Umph!' said the Brown Man.

The next morning as they were sitting at the breakfast table together, Nora plucked up a heart and asked leave to go to see her mother. The Brown Man, who ate nothing, looked at her in a way that made her think he knew all. She felt her spirit die away within her.

'If you only want to see your mother,' said he, 'there is no occasion for your going home. I will bring her to you here. I didn't marry you to be keeping you gadding.'

The Brown Man then went out and whistled for his dog and his horse. They both came; and in a very few minutes they pulled up at the old widow's cabin door.

The poor woman was very glad to see her son-in-law, though she did not know what could bring him so soon.

'Your daughter sends her love to you, Mother,' says the Brown Man, the villain, 'and she'd be obliged to you for a *loan* of a *shoot* of your best clothes, as she's going to give a grand party, and the dressmaker has disappointed her.'

'To be sure and welcome,' said the mother; and making up a bundle of the clothes, she put them into his hands.

'Whogh! whogh!' said the horse as they drove off, 'that was well done. Are we to have a mail of her?'

'Easy, ma-coppuleen, and you'll get your 'nough before night,' said the Brown Man, 'and you likewise, my little dog.'

'Boh!' cried the dog, 'I'm in no hurry – I hunted down a doe this morning that was fed with milk from the horns of the moon.'

Often in the course of that day did Nora Guare go to the door and cast her eye over the weary flat before it, to discern, if possible, the distant figures of her bridegroom and mother. The dusk of the second evening found her alone in the desolate cot. She listened to every sound. At length the door opened, and an old woman, dressed in a jew *jock*, and leaning on a staff, entered the hut. 'O Mother, are you come?' said Nora, and was about to rush into her arms, when the old woman stopped her.

'Whisht! whisht! my child! – I only stepped in before the man to know how you like him? Speak softly, in dread he'd hear you – he's turning the horse loose in the swamp abroad over.'

'O Mother, Mother! such a story!'

'Whisht! easy again – how does he use you?'

'Sarrow worse. That straw my bed, and them white-eyes – and bad ones they are – all my diet. And 'tisn't that same, only – '

41

'Whisht! easy, agin! He'll hear you, may be – well?'

'I'd be easy enough only for his own doings. Listen, Mother. The fusht night, I came about twelve o'clock –'

'Easy, speak easy, eroo!'

'He got up at the call of the horse and the dog and staid out a good hour. He ate nothing next day. The second night, and the second day, it was the same story. The third – '

'Husht! husht! Well, the third night?'

'The third night I said I'd watch him. Mother, don't hold my hand so hard – He got up, and I got up after him – Oh, don't laugh, Mother, for 'tis frightful – I followed him to Mucruss churchyard – Mother, Mother, you hurt my hand – I looked in at the gate – there was great moonlight there, and I could see everything as plain as day.'

'Well, darling – husht! softly! What did you see?'

'My husband by the grave, and the horse, – Turn your head aside, Mother, for your breath is very hot – and the dog and they eating. – Ah, you are not my mother!' shrieked the miserable girl, as the Brown Man flung off his disguise and stood before her, grinning worse than a blacksmith's face through a horse collar. He just looked at her one moment, and then darted his long fingers into her bosom, from which the red blood spouted in so many streams. She was very soon out of all pain, and a merry supper the horse, the dog, and the Brown Man had that night, by all accounts.

From MY LOVE, MY UMBRELLA
by John McGahern

Our lips moved on the saliva of our mouths as I slowly undid the coat button. I tried to control the trembling so as not to tear the small white buttons of the blouse. Coat, blouse, brassiere as names of places on a road. I globed the warm soft breasts in hands. I leaned across the cold metal above the imitation leather she held in her hands to take the small nipples gently in teeth, the steady beat on the umbrella broken by irregular splashes from the branches.

Will she let me? I was afraid as I lifted the woollen skirt; and slowly I moved hands up the soft insides of the thighs, and instead of the 'No' I feared and waited for, the handle became a hard pressure as she pressed on my lips.

I could no longer control the trembling as I felt the sheen on the knickers, I drew them down to her knees, and parted the lips to touch the juices. She hung on my lips. She twitched as the fingers went deeper. She was a virgin.

A memory of the cow pumping on the rubbered arm of the inseminator as the thick juice falls free and he injects the semen with the glass plunger came with a desire to hurt. 'It hurts,' the cold metal touched my face, the rain duller on the sodden cloth by now.

'I won't hurt you,' I said, and pumped low between her thighs, lifting high the coat and skirt so that the seed fell free into the mud and rain, and after resting on each other's mouth I replaced the clothes.

Under the umbrella, one foot asleep, we walked past the small iron railings of the garden towards her room, and at the gate I left her with, 'Where will we meet again?'

We would meet at eight against the radiators inside the Metropole.

We met against those silver radiators three evenings every week for long. We went to cinemas or sat in pubs, it was the course of our love, and as it always rained we made love under the umbrella beneath the same trees in the same way. They say the continuance of sexuality is due to the penis having no memory, and mine each evening spilt its seed into the mud and decomposing leaves as if it was always for the first time.

Sometimes we told each other stories.

The Profane

BUT THE PRODIGAL AND THE OUTRAGEOUS are not what
the sovereigns of the land like to emphasize. Love
becomes refined, noble, almost a patriotic thing. Reading
of the Chinese custom in which the bride rolls out the
scroll and studies the love positions is as remote from
Ireland as those two lands are from each other. Irish love
got wrapped in a shroud that could be called mystery,
mysticism, shame, God, guilt, the Devil or plain flounder.
Stories abound of women deflowered with their corsets
and stockings on, with relics hanging from their person or
their rosary beads dangling from their asensual hands, the
act itself becoming an execution of piety and national
feeling. The surging battle and the cattle forays are one
thing but the bed is quite another.

In nineteen hundred and eight when James Joyce,
arrogant, dedicated and impecunious, was walking the
barley fields and the slob lands, inhaling the gay sweet air of
his native Dublin and inducing the sea wind up his hole, the
National Yearbook was telling him and all others that every
thinking Gael must realize that their predecessors had skill
unrivalled, art untramelled, life unfettered, nationality in its
fullest freedom and that the nation had reached the highest

pinnacle of culture and of fame. Little did they know that Mr Joyce was going to turn that upside down and blast their piety and their nicety, as the following piece from a draft of *Finnegan's Wake*, shows.

From ANNA LIVIA PLURABELLE
The Making of a Chapter
edited by Fred H. Higginson

Tell me, tell me, how did she come through all her fellows, [the daredevil]? Who was the first that ever burst? [Someone it was, whoever you are. Tinker, tailor, soldier, sailor, Paul pry or polishman] That's [the] thing I always [want] to know. [Well, she can't put her hand on him for the moment]. She says herself she hardly knew who he was or what he did or [when] he crossed her. She was [just] a young thin pale slip of a thing then [sauntering] and he was a heavy lurching [liea-broad] Curraghman [making hay for the sun to shine] as strong as the oaks there used to [grow] that time in killing Kildare that first fell across her. You're wrong there. You're all wrong. It was ages [long] before that in the county Wicklow, the garden of Erin, before she ever dreamt she'd end in the barleyfields and pennylands of Humphreystown and lie with a landleaper, well on the wane. Wast it, was it? Are you sure? Where in Wicklow? Tell me where, the very first time! I will if you listen. You know the [hazel dell of] Lugge-law? Well, there once dwelt [a local hermit named Michael Orkney and] one day in [warm] June so young and shy and so limber she looked, [the kind of curves you simply can't stop feeling], he plunged both of his blessed [anointed] hands up to his wrists in [the streams of] her hair that was rich red

48

like [the] brown bog. And he couldn't help [it], thirst was too hot for him, [he had to forget the monk in the man] he cooled his lips in smiling mood kiss after kiss [on] Anna Livia's freckled cheek. O, wasn't he the bold priest! [And] wasn't she the naughty [Livvy]! Naughtynaughty is her name. Two lads in their breeches went through her before that, Barefoot Byrne and Billy Wade, [Lugnaquilla's noble pair] before she had a hint of [a] hair there to hide and ere that again she was licked by a hound [while] doing her pee, sweet and simple, on the side of [the] hill [of old Kippure] in [birdsong and] shearing time but first of all, worst of all, she [sideslipped out by] a gap [in the devil's glen] when [her] nurse was [sound] asleep [in a sloot] and fell before she found her stride [and lay] and wriggled under a [fallow] cow.

From ENCOUNTER
translated by Patrick Power

[Iubhdan, the king of the little people, and Bebo his wife, are brought into the presence of the king of Ulster, Fergus. Iubhdan introduces himself and his queen.]

Said Fergus: 'Take him out to the common household and hold him carefully.' Iubhdan was brought out after that and Bebo was left inside with Fergus and he fell in love with her and made love to her. When he was having intercourse with her he placed his hand on the top of her head. The queen inquired why he did this. 'I shouldn't be surprised,' said he, 'if my penis which is seven fists long, didn't go through your head and you only three fists high. For that reason I put my hand on your head.'

'Desist from it Fergus,' said the queen, 'it's many a thing that a woman's loins absorb.'

Fergus went then to where Iubhdan was. 'I went into your wife, Iubhdan,' said Fergus.

'She liked that,' said Iubhdan.

'I went again,' said Fergus.

'You enjoyed that,' said Iubhdan.

'I went the third time,' said he.

'Both of you liked that,' said Iubhdan.

'I went into her a fourth time,' said Fergus.

'Shit in her from this out! If you'd care to do me some good,' said Iubhdan, 'don't leave me among these people here. The breath of the big men is making a corrupt corpse of me....'

From THE MIDNIGHT COURT
by Bryan Merriman, translated by Frank O'Connor

A man that's looking for a wife,
Here's a face that will keep for life!
Hand and arm and neck and breast,
Each is better than the rest.
Look at that waist! My legs are long,
Limber as willows and light and strong,
There's bottom and belly that claim attention
And the best concealed that I needn't mention.

From THE LAND OF COCKAIGNE
Anon

The young monks each day
After meat, go out to play:
Despite their sleeves and cowl
There is no hawk or swift fowl
Faster flying through the sky
Than these monks when feeling high.
When the abbot sees them flee,
He follows them with glee,
But nevertheless bids the throng
To alight for evensong.
When the monks don't come down,
But further flee, at random,
He takes a maiden, from the mass,
And turning up her plump white ass,
Beats the tabours with his hand,
To make his monks alight to land.
The monks, all seeing that,
Drop from the sky, upon the dot,
And ring the wench all about
To thwack her white toute,
And after this pleasant work
Wend meekly home to drink
Going to their collation
In a goodly fair procession.

Another abbey is thereby –
Forsooth, a great fair nunnery,
Up a river of sweet milk,
Where there is surplus of silk.
When the summer sun is hot,
The young nuns take a boat
And sail upon that river,
Both with oars and rudder.

When they are far from the abbey
They strip themselves naked to play,
And leaping down into the brim
Set themselves skilfully to swim.
The monks, when they this espy,
Rise up, and forthwith fly
And coming to the nuns anon
Each monk grabs him one
And quickly bears forth his prey
To the great, grey abbey,
And teaches the nuns an orison
With jigging up and down.

He that would be a stallion good
And can set straight his hood,
That monk shall have, without fear,
Twelve new wives each year,
While the monk who sleeps the best
And above all, likes his rest,
There is hope for him, Got wot,
Soon to be a father abbot.

THE BLAMELESS LECHER
translated by Donncha O Corrain and John Montague

Now that I'm sent from the North,
Kenneth, do tell me my crime;
for I'd never do with fine ladies
what I wouldn't do with my wife.

A greybeard accused me – God help him –
of having to do with his dear,
but I'd no more lift up her skirt
than a cat would lap up the cream,

than a stag would clear a high hedge
than a salmon leap from the stream,
than a woman play mischievous tricks:
or I fill a fine horn for my beer.

Even if she begged, I wouldn't
against her good man's word –
no more than the bear seeks honey
or the big boar commands his herd.

So they've charged me with a trifle,
easy Gormlaith from Ath Da Rinn –
that I held her crooked in my arm
as she moved her lecherous limbs.

If we were straying together
on that green grassy walk
and her lips happened on mine:
is that great matter for talk?

I am an innocent man:
gentle Kenneth falsely thinks
that I swived his noble lady
because we shared a quiet drink.

The Desperate

LOVE SUNDERED IS, as Sean O'Casey would say a 'darlin'
thing. Certainly it is fertile and allows for much more
rumination. It lives by an energy of the mind that gives it
an existence that is stronger and more indestructible than
if it were real. It becomes a super reality while also
remaining a figment. And for a race as committed to loss
as we are, the murdered love, the deprived love, the
absent love, the impossible love and the love reserved for
eternity, these take precedence.

> Oh! I would ask no happier bed
> Than the chill wave my love lies under
> Sweeter to rest together, dead,
> Far sweeter than to live asunder.

AILEEN AROON
translated by Gerald Griffin

When, like the early rose,
    Aileen aroon!
Beauty in childhood blows,
    Aileen aroon!
When, like a diadem,
Buds blush around the stem,
Which is the fairest gem?
    Aileen aroon!

Is it the laughing eye?
    Aileen aroon!
Is it the timid sigh?
    Aileen aroon!
Is it the tender tone,
Soft as the stringed harp's moan?
Oh, is it truth alone?
    Aileen aroon!

When, like the rising day,
    Aileen aroon!
Love sends his early ray,
    Aileen aroon!
What makes his dawning glow
Changeless through joy or woe?
Only the constant know,
    Aileen aroon!

I know a valley fair,
    Aileen aroon!
I knew a cottage there,
    Aileen aroon!
Far in that valley's shade
I knew a gentle maid,

Flower of the hazel glade,
              Aileen aroon!

Who in the song so sweet?
              Aileen aroon!
Who in the dance so sweet?
              Aileen aroon!
Dear were her charms to me,
Dearer her laughter free,
Dearest her constancy,
              Aileen aroon!

Were she no longer true,
              Aileen aroon!
What should her lover do?
              Aileen aroon!
Fly with his broken chain
Far o'er the sounding main,
Never to love again,
              Aileen aroon!

Youth must with time decay,
              Aileen aroon!
Beauty must fade away,
              Aileen aroon!
Castles are sacked in war,
Chieftains are scattered far,
Truth is a fixed star,
              Aileen aroon!

The name of Deirdre is one associated with love and lament.
It could be said that her own beauty wrought it:

From THE EXILE OF THE SONS OF USNACH
translated by A. H. Leahy

Now once it chanced upon a certain day in the time of winter that the foster-father of Deirdre had employed himself in skinning a calf upon the snow, in order to prepare a roast for her, and the blood of the calf lay upon the snow, and she saw a black raven come down to drink it. And 'Levorcham,' said Deirdre, 'that man only will I love, who hath the three colours that I see here, his hair as black as the raven, his cheeks red like the blood, and his body as white as the snow.' 'Dignity and good fortune to thee!' said Levorcham; 'that man is not far away. Yonder is he in the burg which is nigh; and the name of him is Naisi, the son of Usnach.' 'I shall never be in good health again,' said Deirdre, 'until the time come when I may see him.'

It befell that Naisi was upon a certain day alone upon the rampart of the burg of Emain, and he sent his warrior-cry with music abroad: well did the musical cry ring out that was raised by the sons of Usnach. Each cow and every beast that heard them, gave of milk two-thirds more than its wont; and each man by whom that cry was heard deemed it to be fully joyous, and a dear pleasure to him. Goodly moreover was the play that these men made with their weapons; if the whole province of Ulster had been assembled together against them in one place, and they three only had been able to set their backs against one another, the men of Ulster would not have borne away victory from those three; so well were they skilled in parry and defence. And they were swift of foot when they hunted the game, and with them it was the custom to chase the quarry to its death.

Now when this Naisi found himself alone on the plain, Deirdre also soon escaped outside her house to him, and she ran past him, and at first he knew not who she might be.

'Fair is the young heifer that springs past me!' he cried.

'Well may the young heifers be great,' she said, 'in a place where none may find a bull.'

'Thou hast, as thy bull,' said he, 'the bull of the whole province of Ulster, even Conor the king of Ulster.'

'I would choose between you two,' she said, 'and I would take for myself a younger bull, even such as thou art.'

'Not so, indeed,' said Naisi, 'for I fear the prophecy of Cathbad.'

'Sayest thou this, as meaning to refuse me?' said she.

'Yea indeed,' he said; and she sprang upon him, and she seized him by his two ears. 'Two ears of shame and of mockery shalt thou have,' she cried, 'if thou take me not with thee.'

'Release me, O my wife!' said he.

'That will I.'

Then Naisi raised his musical warrior-cry, and the men of Ulster heard it, and each of them one after another sprang up: and the sons of Usnach hurried out in order to hold back their brother.

'What is it,' they said, 'that thou dost? let it not be by any fault of thine that war is stirred up between us and the men of Ulster.'

Then he told them all that he had done; and 'There shall evil come on thee from this,' said they; 'moreover thou shalt lie under the reproach of shame so long as thou dost live; and we will go with her into another land, for there is no king in all Ireland who will refuse us welcome if we come to him.'

Then they took counsel together, and that same night they departed, three times fifty warriors, and the same number of women, and dogs, and servants, and Deirdre went with them. And for a long time they wandered about Ireland, in homage to this man or that; and often Conor sought to slay them, either by ambuscade or by treachery; from round about Assaroe, near to Ballyshannon in the west, they journeyed, and they turned them back to Benn Etar, in the northeast, which men today call the Mountain of Howth. Nevertheless the men of Ulster drave them from the land, and they came to the land of Alba, and in its wildernesses they dwelled. And when the chase of the wild beasts of the mountains failed them, they made foray upon the cattle of the men of Alba, and took them for themselves; and the men of Alba gathered themselves together with intent to destroy them. Then they took shelter with the king of Alba, and the king took them into his following, and they served him in war. And they made for themselves houses of their own in the meadows by the king's burg: it was on account of Deirdre that these houses were made, for they feared that men might see her, and that on her account they might be slain.

Now one day the high-steward of the king went out in the early morning, and he made a cast about Naisi's house, and saw those two sleeping therein, and he hurried back to the king, and awaked him: 'We have,' said he, 'up to this day found no wife for thee of like dignity to thyself. Naisi the son of Usnach hath a wife of worth sufficient for the emperor of the western world! Let Naisi be slain, and let his wife share thy couch.'

'Not so!' said the king, 'but do thou prepare thyself to go each day to her house, and woo her for me secretly.'

Thus was it done; but Deirdre, whatsoever the steward told her, was accustomed straightway to recount it each evening to her spouse; and since nothing was obtained from her, the sons of Usnach were sent into dangers, and into wars, and into strifes that thereby they might be overcome. Nevertheless they showed themselves to be stout in every strife, so that no advantage did the king gain from them by such attempts as these.

The men of Alba were gathered together to destroy the sons of Usnach, and this also was told to Deirdre. And she told her news to Naisi: 'Depart hence!' said she, 'for if ye depart not this night, upon the morrow ye shall be slain!' And they marched away that night, and they betook themselves to an island of the sea.

Now the news of what had passed was brought to the men of Ulster. ' 'Tis pity, O Conor!' said they, 'that the sons of

Usnach should die in the land of foes, for the sake of an evil woman. It is better that they should come under thy protection and that the (fated) slaying should be done here and that they should come into their own land, rather than that they should fall at the hands of foes.' 'Let them come to us then,' said Conor, 'and let men go as securities to them.' The news was brought to them.

'This is welcome news for us,' they said; 'we will indeed come, and let Fergus come as our surety, and Dubhtach, and Cormac the son of Conor.' These then went to them, and they moved them to pass over the sea.

But at the contrivance of Conor, Fergus was pressed to join in an ale-feast, while the sons of Usnach were pledged to eat no food in Erin, until they had eaten the food of Conor. So Fergus tarried behind with Dubhtach and Cormac; and the sons of Usnach went on, accompanied by Fiacha, Fergus' son; until they came to the meadows around Emain.

Now at that time Eogan the son of Durthacht had come to Emain to make his peace with Conor, for they had for a long time been at enmity; and to him, and to the warmen of Conor, the charge was given that they should slay the sons of Usnach, in order that they should not come before the king. The sons of Usnach stood upon the level part of the meadows, and the women sat upon the ramparts of Emain. And Eogan came with his warriors across the meadow, and the son of Fergus took his place by Naisi's side. And Eogan greeted them with a mighty thrust of his spear, and the spear brake Naisi's back in sunder, and passed through it. The son of Fergus made a spring, and he threw both arms around Naisi, and he brought him beneath himself to shelter him, while he threw himself down above him; and it was thus that Naisi was slain, through the body of the son of Fergus. Then there began a murder throughout the meadow, so that none escaped who did not fall by the points of the spears, or the edge of the sword, and Deirdre was brought to Conor to be in his power, and her arms were bound behind her back.
... Deirdre lived on for a year in the household of Conor;

and during all that time she smiled no smile of laughter; she satisfied not herself with food or with sleep, and she raised not her head from her knee. . . .

'Whom dost thou hate the most,' said Conor, 'of these whom thou now seest?'

'Thee thyself,' she answered, 'and with thee, Eogan the son of Durthacht.'

'Then,' said Conor, 'thou shalt dwell with Eogan for a year;' and he gave Deirdre over into Eogan's hand.

Now upon the morrow they went away over the festal plain of Macha, and Deirdre sat behind Eogan in the chariot; and the two who were with her were the two men whom she would never willingly have seen together upon the earth, and as she looked upon them, 'Ha, Deirdre,' said Conor, 'it is the same glance that a ewe gives when between two rams that thou sharest now between me and Eogan!' Now there was a great rock of stone in front of them, and Deirdre struck her head upon that stone, and she shattered her head, and so she died.

Not all the heroines lost in such a queenly way. Some speak with the uncanny simplicity of the innocent, and some like the near-demented:

UP AT GORTHACARNAUN
traditional folk-song

A hundred farewells to last night (Oh, alas!)
That this night is not still quite new,
With the sportive young swain
Who would coax me so nicely on his knee.
Since you made me refuse (you)
Oh, darling! my love is not yours;
But a hundred times pity,
The hills stand between me and you.

This garden is grown wild,
My fair love! and I am not alone.
The posies now grow there,
The finest that ever you saw.
No music of harps will be heard
Going this way, nor the sweet song of birds,
Since he stole away over the sea
The fair branch to Castle O'Neill.

Oh! it is in Castle O'Neill
Dwells the pearl that took from me my love;
To him I myself gave affection,
Unknown to the world, 'tis my grief!
'Tis at the hearth of the big house
My love has his dwelling and sleeps.
His like there is not to be found,
The star of knowledge in that town beyond.

I would think your little kiss sweeter
Than the rose that springs from the bud.
And with loneliness after my love
I hardly can sleep at all.
A year ago unto last night,
The horses burst out through the hedge.

And they went of a leap,
Alas! out into the flood.

There is no tide, howe'er great,
But it comes in a while to ebb,
They are all only deceivers,
And it can't be but my love will return.

OH, GENTLE YOUTH
traditional folk-song

Ah! gentle young man, where slept you last night?
On the side of your bed, and you heeded me not.
Did you know my affliction not a wink you'd have slept,
'Twas your bier going the way, left this pang in my side.

When I rise in the morning my prayer is a tear.
When I lie on my bed 'tis sadly I moan;
My hair is now falling, and going like the mist,
And through grief for you, darling, I shall not long live.

I will hoist my sails for Joyce country at early morning,
To visit my thousand treasures, and home I shall never
   return.
What matters to me what any one says, when my love
   says not a word?
But if we were born for each other, all Ireland would not
   separate us.

I would prefer a useful man, in autumn-time or spring,
Who would cut for me the barley, and tie it up in
                    sheaves.
I'd far prefer a young boy, were he only to make my
                    bed,
Than the riches of George in coaches, along with an old
                    widower.

THE BETRAYAL
by Alice Furlong

When you were weary, roaming the wide world over,
I gave my fickle heart to a new lover.
Now they tell me that you are lying dead:
O mountains fall on me and hide my head!

When you lay burning in the throes of fever,
He vowed me love by the willow-margined river:
Death smote you there – here was your trust betrayed,
O darkness, cover me, I am afraid!

Yea, in the hour of your supremest trial,
I laughed with him! The shadow on the dial
Stayed not, aghast at my dread ignorance:
Nor man nor angel looked at me askance.

Under the mountains there is peace abiding,
Darkness shall be pavilion for my hiding,
Tears shall blot out the sin of broken faith,
The lips that falsely kissed, shall kiss but Death.

From THE REAL CHARLOTTE
by E. Œ. Somerville and Martin Ross

On this golden, still afternoon, Francie strayed out soon after lunch, half dazed with unhappiness and excitement. To-night her husband would come home. In four days Hawkins would have gone, as eternally, so far as she was concerned, as if he were dead; he would soon forget her, she thought, as she walked to and fro among the blossoming apple trees, in the kitchen-garden. Men forgot very easily, and thanks to the way she had tried her best to make him think she didn't care, there was not a word of hers to bring him back to her. She hated herself for her discretion; her soul thirsted for even one word of understanding, that would be something to live upon in future days of abnegation, when it would be nothing to her that she had gained his respect, and one tender memory would be worth a dozen self-congratulations.

She turned at the end of the walk and came back again under the apple trees; the ground under her feet was white with fallen blossoms; her fair hair gleamed among the thick embroidery of the branches, and her face was not shamed by their translucent pink and white. At a little distance Eliza Hackett, in a starched lilac calico, was gathering spinach, and meditating no doubt with comfortable assurance on the legitimacy of Father Heffernan's apostolic succession, but outwardly the embodiment of solid household routine and respectability. As Francie passed her she raised her decorous face from the spinach-bed with a question as to whether the trout would be for dinner or for breakfast; the master always fancied fish for his breakfast, she reminded Francie. Eliza Hackett's tone was distant, but admonitory, and it dispelled in a moment the visions of another now impossible future that were holding high carnival before Francie's vexed eyes. The fetter made itself coldly felt, and following came the quick pang of remorse at the thought of the man who was wasting on her the best love he had to give. Her change of mood was headlong, but its only possible expression was trivial to absurdity, if indeed any incident in a soul's struggle can be called trivial. Some day, further on in eternity, human beings will know what their standards of proportion and comparison are worth, and may perhaps find the glory of some trifling actions almost insufferable.

She gave the necessary order, and hurrying into the house brought out from it the piece of corduroy that she was stitching in lines of red silk as a waistcoat for her husband, and with a childish excitement at the thought of this expiation, took the path that led to the shrubbery on the hill. As she reached its first turn she hesitated and stopped, an idea of further and fuller renunciation occurring to her. Turning, she called to the figure stooping among the glossy rows of spinach to desire that the parlour-maid should say that this afternoon she was not at home. Had Eliza Hackett then and there obeyed the order, it is possible that many things would have happened differently. But fate is seldom without a second string to her bow, and even if Francie's message had not been delayed by Eliza Hackett's determination to gather a pint of green gooseberries before she went in, it is possible that Hawkins would, none the less, have found his way to the top of the shrubbery, where Francie was sewing with the assiduity of Penelope. It was about four o'clock when she heard his step coming up the devious slants of the path, and she knew as she heard it that, in spite of all her precautions, she had expected him. His manner and even his look had nothing now in them of the confident lover of last year; his flippancy was gone, and when he began by reproaching her for having hidden from him, his face was angry and wretched, and he spoke like a person who had been seriously and unjustly hurt. He was more in love than he had ever been before, and he was taking it badly, like a fever that the chills of opposition were driving back into his system.

She made excuses as best she might, with her eyes bent upon her work.

'I might have been sitting in the drawing-room now,' he

said petulantly; 'only that Miss Mullen had seen you going off here by yourself, and told me I'd better go and find you.'

An unreasoning fear came over Francie, a fear as of something uncanny.

'Let us go back to the house,' she said; 'Charlotte will be expecting us.' She said it to contradict the thought that had become definite for the first time. 'Come; I'm going in.'

Hawkins did not move. 'I suppose you forget that this is Wednesday, and that I'm going on Saturday,' he replied dully. 'In any case you'll not be much good to Charlotte. She's gone up to pack her things. She told me herself she was going to be very busy, as she had to start at six o'clock.'

Francie leaned back, and realized that now she had no one to look to but herself, and happiness and misery fought within her till her hands trembled as she worked.

Each knew that this was, to all intents and purposes, their last meeting, and their consciousness was charged to brimming with unexpressed farewell. She talked of indifferent subjects: of what Aldershot would be like, of what Lismoyle would think of the new regiment, of the trouble that he would have in packing his pictures, parrying, with a weakening hand, his efforts to make every subject personal; and all the time the laburnum drooped in beautiful despair above her, as if listening and grieving, and the cool-leaved lilac sent its fragrance to mingle with her pain, and to stir her to rebellion with the ecstasy of spring-time. The minutes passed barrenly by, and as has been said, the silences became longer and more clinging, and the thoughts that filled them made each successive subject more bare and artificial. At last Hawkins got up, and walking to the opening cut in the shrubs, stood, with his hands in his pockets, looking out at the lake and the mountains. Francie stitched on; it seemed to her that if she stopped she would lose her last hold upon herself; she felt as if her work were a talisman to remind her of all the things that she was in peril of forgetting. When, that night, she took up the waistcoat again to work at it, she thought that her heart's blood had gone into the red stitches.

It was several minutes before Hawkins spoke.

'Francie,' he said, turning round and speaking thickly, 'are you going to let me leave you in this – in this kind of way? Have you realized that when I go on Saturday it's most likely – it's pretty certain, in fact – that we shall never see each other again?'

'Yes, I have,' she said, after a pause of a second or two. She did not say that for a fortnight her soul had beaten itself against the thought, and that to hear it in words was as much as her self-command could bear.

'You seem to care a great deal!' he said violently; 'you're thinking of nothing but that infernal piece of work, that I loathe the very sight of. Don't you think you could do without it for five minutes, at all events?'

She let her hands drop into her lap, but made no other reply.

'You're not a bit like what you used to be. You seem to take a delight in snubbing me and shutting me up. I must say, I never thought you'd have turned into a prig!' He felt this reproach to be so biting that he paused upon it to give it its full effect. 'Here I am going to England in four days, and to India in four months, and it's ten to one if I ever come home again. I mean to volunteer for the very first row that turns up. But it's just the same to you, you won't even take the trouble to say you're sorry.'

'If you had taken the trouble to answer my letters last autumn, you wouldn't be saying these things to me now,' she said, speaking low and hurriedly.

'I don't believe it! I believe if you had cared about me then you wouldn't treat me like this now.'

'I *did* care for you,' she said, while the hard-held tears forced their way to her eyes; 'you made me do it, and then you threw me over, and now you're trying to put the blame on me!'

He saw the glisten on her eyelashes, and it almost took from him the understanding of what she said.

'Francie,' he said, his voice shaking, and his usually confident eyes owning the infection of her tears, 'you might forget that. I'm miserable. I can't bear to leave you!' He sat down again beside her, and catching her hand, kissed it with a passion of repentance. He felt it shrink from his lips, but the touch of it had intoxicated him, and suddenly she was in his arms.

For a speechless instant they clung to each other; her head dropped to his shoulder, as if the sharp release from the tension of the last fortnight had killed her, and the familiar voice murmured in her ear:

'Say it to me – say you love me.'

'Yes I do – my dearest – ' she said, with a moan that was tragically at variance with the confession. 'Ah, why do you make me so wicked!' She snatched herself away from him, and stood up, trembling all over. 'I wish I had never seen you – I wish I was dead.'

'I don't care what you say now,' said Hawkins, springing to his feet, 'you've said you loved me, and I know you mean it. Will you stand by it?' he went on wildly. 'If you'll only say the word I'll chuck everything overboard – I can't go away from you like this. Once I'm in England I can't get back here, and if I did, what good would it be to me? He'd never give us a chance of seeing each other, and we'd both be more miserable than we are, unless – unless there was a chance of meeting you in Dublin or somewhere – ?' He stopped for an instant. Francie mutely shook her head. 'Well, then, I shall never see you.'

There was silence, and the words settled down into both their hearts. He cursed himself for being afraid of her, she whom he had always felt to be his inferior, yet when he spoke it was with an effort.

'Come away with me out of this – come away with me for good and all! What's the odds? We can't be more than happy!'

Francie made an instinctive gesture with her hand while he spoke, as if to stop him, but she said nothing, and almost immediately the distant rush and rattle of a train came quietly into the stillness.

'That's his train!' she exclaimed, looking as startled as if the sound had been a sign from heaven. 'Oh, go away! He mustn't meet you coming away from here.'

'I'll go if you give me a kiss,' he answered drunkenly. His arms were round her again, when they dropped to his side as if he had been shot.

There was a footstep on the path immediately below the lilac bushes, and Charlotte's voice called to Francie that she was just starting for home and had come to make her adieux.

From THREE WOMEN WHO WEPT
by James Stephens

And then he went away. She did not see him any more. He was not by the waterfall on the Dodder, nor hanging over the bear-pit in the zoo. He was not in the Chapel, nor on the pavement when she came out of a shop. He was not anywhere. She searched, but he was not anywhere. And the sun became the hot pest it had always been: the heavens were stuffed with dirty clouds the way a secondhand shop is stuffed with dirty bundles: the trees were hulking corner-boys with muddy boots: the wind blew dust into her eye, and her brothers pulled her hair and kicked her hat; so that she went apart from all these. She sat before the mirror regarding herself with woeful amazement –

'He was afraid of me!' she said.

And she wept into his monstrous handkerchief.

THE NOBLE LAY OF AILLINN
translated by Stopford A. Brooke

Prince Bailè of Ulster rode out in the morn
To meet his love at the ford;
And he loved her better than lands or life,
And dearer than his sword.

And she was Aillinn, fair as the sea,
The Prince of Leinster's daughter,
And she longed for him more than a wounded man,
Who sees death, longs for water.

They sent a message each to each:
'Oh, meet me near or far;'
And the ford divided the kingdoms two,
And the kings were both at war.

And the Prince came first to the water's pass,
And oh, he thought no ill:
When he saw with pain a great grey man
Come striding o'er the hill.

His cloak was the ragged thunder-cloud,
And his cap the whirling snow,
And his eyes were the lightning in the storm,
And his horn he 'gan to blow.

'What news, what news, thou great grey man?
I fear 'tis ill with me.'
'Oh, Aillinn is dead, and her lips are cold,
And she died for loving thee.'

And he looked and saw no more the man,
But a trail of driving rain.
'Woe! woe!' he cried, and took his sword
And drave his heart in twain.

And out of his blood burst forth a spring,
And a yew-tree out of his breast,
And it grew so deep, and it grew so high,
The doves came there to rest.

But Aillinn was coming to keep her tryst,
The hour her lover fell;
And she rode as fast as the western wind
Across the heathery hill.

Behind her flew her loosened hair,
Her happy heart did beat;
When she was 'ware of a cloud of storm
Came driving down the street.

And out of it stepped a great grey man,
And his cap was peaked with snow;
The fire of death was in his eyes,
And he 'gan his horn to blow.

'What news, what news, thou great grey man?
And is it ill to me?'
'Oh, Bailè the Prince is dead at the ford,
And he died for loving thee.'

Pale, pale she grew, and two large tears
Dropped down like heavy rain,
And she fell to earth with a woeful cry,
For she broke her heart in twain.

And out of her tears two fountains rose
That watered all the ground,
And out of her heart an apple-tree grew
That heard the water's sound.

Oh, woe were the kings, and woe were the queens,
And woe were the people all;

And the poets sang their love and their death
In cottage and in hall.

And the men of Ulster a tablet made
From the wood of Bailè's tree,
And the men of Leinster did the like
Of Aillinn's apple-tree.

And on the one the poets wrote
The lover-tales of Leinster,
And on the other all the deeds
That lover wrought in Ulster.

Now when a hundred years had gone
The King of all the land
Kept a feast at Tara, and he bade
His poets sing a strand.

They sang the sweet unhappy tale,
The noble Aillinn's lay.
'Go, bring the tablets,' cried the King,
'For I have wept today.'

But when he held in his right hand
The wood of Bailè's tree
And in his left the tablet smooth
From Aillin's apple-tree,

The lovers in the wood who kept
Love-longing ever true,
Knew one another, and at once
From the hands of the King they flew.

As ivy to the oak they clung,
Their kiss no man could sever –
Oh, joy for lovers parted long
To meet, at last, for ever!

POEM IX
by Gormlaith, translated by Osborn Bergin

Heavy to-night is my sighing, O God! It is heavier to-day than yesterday. Through grief for the son of bright Niall Glúndubh I desire to go alive into the earth.

My friends grow fewer and fewer, since I no more have sight of Niall: my fair bright ear hears nothing at which I laugh.

Dead is my father, dead my mother, dead are my two brothers, dead my fosterer, honoured and revered, dead my two fosterbrothers.

Dead alas! is Dubh Chabhlaigh the just, who would set me upon a golden vat, and would give me no morsel without honey, Dubh Chabhlaigh of fair bright skin.

Dead the son of the king of Innsi Gall, he the son of Amhlaeibh of Arann; Amhlaeibh's son used to be on ... of my fair knee like a beloved son.

Though all these have gone from the glorious yellow-topped earth, sorer to me is it that dear Domhnall should be one night under the earth.

Though bitter every sickness and strife that is given to living man, the child that is born of one's fair body, that is what lives in one's mind.

Had I sent my darling to the men of Meath, the race of upright Colmán would have guarded and kept my lad.

Alas for her who entrusts to a foolish woman the keeping of her tender child, since the protection of life should be enjoined upon a king's son or a royal heir.

Woe to her who allowed the gentle sweet-voiced lad to go into Uí Fiachrach, a land where water is plentiful, and men are unruly.

Domhnall son of Niall Glúndubh the bright, son of Aed Finnliath of Febhal, son of Niall Caille – motionless! – son of noble Aed Oirdnide.

Son of Niall Frasach from Ráith Mór, who bestowed honour upon poets, son of Fergal who was prince of Femen, son of hospitable Mael Dúin.

Son of Mael Fithrigh, son of Aed, son of Domhnall the generous and comely, son of Muirchertach the Great from the plain, son of Muiredach, son of Eogan.

Son of Niall of the Nine Hostages, the festive, son of Eochaidh Muighmheadhón: the grandmother of dear Domhnall was daughter of Alpin from Scotland.

There is the pedigree of my own son, whose death darkens the sun. White was his neck, white his foot. My heart has found nought so heavy.

LIGHT LOVE
translated by Robin Flower

Out of sight is out of mind,
Maids no loyal faith maintain;
Light love goes ranging and always changing
Like a shifting April's sun and rain.

You were mine a year ago,
Love this year is fled away;
And that bright weather we knew together
Is clouded over since yesterday.

Ne'er a woman loves me now,
And my loving days are done;
That one should leave me it does not grieve me,
But women turn from me, every one!

MY GRIEF ON THE SEA
by Douglas Hyde

My grief on the sea,
How the waves of it roll!
For they heave between me
And love of my soul!

Abandoned, forsaken,
To grief and to care,
Will the sea ever waken
Relief from despair?

My grief, and my trouble!
Would he and I were
In the province of Leinster,
Or county of Clare.

Were I and my darling –
Oh, heart-bitter wound! –
On board of the ship
For America bound.

On a green bed of rushes
All last night I lay,
And I flung it abroad
With the heat of the day.

And my love came behind me –
He came from the south;
His breast to my bosom,
His mouth to my mouth.

Killarney Cathedral, County Kerry, Ireland

Llangollen, Clwyd, Wales

The Male

I would like my love to die
and the rain to be falling on the graveyard
and on me walking the streets
mourning she who sought to love me.

Collected Poems
Samuel Beckett

Lovely whore though,
Lovely, lovely whore
And choosy –
Slept with Conn,
Slept with Niall,
Slept with Brian,
Slept with Rory.

Slide then,
The long slide.

Of course it shows

Cathleen
translated by Thomas MacIntyre

In women love begets desire
In men desire begets love.

Dean Swift

Talk to him about himself: then he will love you – to your great alarm.

George Bernard Shaw

> If I had Mary in the wood
> I'd give Mary something good
> If I had Mary in the woods
> I'd keep her there till morning

> On a mossy bank I sat me down, with the maiden
> by my side;
> With gentle words I courted her, and asked her
> to be my bride;
> She said, 'Young man don't bring me blame,'
> and swiftly turned away;
> And the morning light was shining bright,
> at the dawning of the day.

From The Dawning of the Day
traditional folk-song

'Every woman's head is her husband.'

THAT ARROGANCE RUNS LIKE BINDWEED through centuries of swaggering and double-phallused Irish maledom. It was said by King Cormac MacArt to the woman who dreamed that her head had been struck off and that there grew out of her neck a large and stately tree which however was overwhelmed by the sea. Her husband interpreted her vision to mean his death on the morrow and the birth of his son, who would however be eventually strangled by the bone of a fish. But the fact remains that her head, her thought and her dream were his to decipher.

It must be said of course that the women of those times were lustier and more voracious. One, seeing Daghda, the Irish Hercules, was so ready for congress that she had straddled the river and had one foot on the north bank and the other on the south. Defloweration was no delicate thing:

Hardship unfamiliar should she then discover,
　　Not yet by her encountered;
Let her not by coldness, in doing and enduring,
　　Try to shun her trouble.
Many other valleys, likewise, have been plundered,
　　Wounding unforbidden;

David O'Bruadair

Irish men have not been particularly renowned for their cossetting of women. Indeed the Blessed Virgin Mary comes in for odium from them, as devotion to her is thought to be cissyish. The bottle and its ravening aftermath have got between many an Irishman and his sweetheart. Indeed there are women in Ireland who would question the matter and ask if their men loved them at all, or if they had not used them as objects to cohabit with in the dark, and repudiate in the daylight. The Irish honeymoon often includes the bride, the groom and the groom's male cronies. There is no Irish Werther and if there were he would be the laughing stock of the country, his idiocy amplified by that uncanny genius Myles na Gopaleen. Not that the man should be expected to have such finer tendencies, springing as he does from a race where according to Solinus, a second-century pedant, the newborn Irish man child had its first solid nutriment administered by the mother on the point of her husband's sword, while she uttered gentile prayers that upon such a weapon he would eventually and honourably die.

There are of course the later exceptions, those who climbed the lofty tower and celebrated the woman with breasts round, fine and shapely, breasts incidentally that no rude hand had smudged. Mr W.B.Yeats was wracked by the long love of Maud Gonne MacBride and haunted for years afterwards, and Oscar Wilde languished in Reading Gaol waiting insensibly for the love letters that never came.

Dean Swift had both Stella and Vanessa to contend with and while prating to Stella and calling her 'Derichar' or telling her he had a 'cod' he would enjoin Vanessa to seek general society, to take exercise to direct the currents of her passion. Three long weeks she would pine and beg for a message. 'A fig for your letter and messages, adieu,' he would say and having damped her ardour he would amend it or rekindle it with some damned ambiguous note. He of course was in mortal fear of the itch if she or Stella or any other woman were to shake his hand. Shaw also relished the conflict of two women and composed the most beguiling and suggestive letters to Ellen Terry while commandeering the love of the practical *and* prosperous Miss Townshend: 'Miss P.T. [Miss Townshend] is a restful person but plain, a ladylike woman with green eyes,' he would say to Ellen while asking her to choose a nice gamekeeper's cottage with a communicating secret passage. He should have written to D.H. Lawrence. One day he loved Ellen, another day he didn't, the way ardour has it. In the throes he would ask to be beaten, petted, kissed, consoled, but all the time they would avoid meeting, they would shirk temptation, they would transcribe it all onto paper. They understood the delights of indefinite postponement. He could say that there were swords in his heart but they were not murderous ones. Not like those of James Clarence Mangan who because of love tells us that his peace was everlastingly blighted. Deeply and incurably smitten, he avowed his passion and was changed in heart and soul. His bosom burned with a 'lava-flood' but it was only for a bright brief hour. The lady betrayed him. For J.M. Synge it was a different intervention – it was none other than death. To the actress Maire O'Neill he wrote:

Little Heart you dont know how much feeling I have for you. You are like my child, and my little wife, and my good angel, and my greatest friend, all in one! I dont believe there has been a woman in Ireland loved the way I love you for a thousand years.

A VISION
by Tadhg Dall O'Huiginn

Art thou the woman who was here last night with me in a vision? uncertain about thee as I am, thou bright form, my mind is bewildered.

If thou be not she who came before, O slender figure, gentle and soft of hand, and dainty of step, thou art exactly similar.

Thy glowing cheek, thy blue eye – never were there formed from the four-fold element two more similar in form, O yellow, curly, plaited locks.

Thy white teeth, thy crimson lips which make sufficing lullaby, brown brows of the hue of the sloe, and all that lies between them.

Throat like the blossom of the lily, long, slender hands; supple, plump flesh, of the hue of the waves, dulling the whiteness of the river's foam.

Small, smooth, white breasts rising above a lovely, shining slope; gentle expanses, with borders most fair and delightful, they are to be likened to fairy knolls.

On the ends of thy luxuriant tresses are flocks not usual in winter, which have been bathed in pure gold; a most wondrous flock.

I am worthy of trust, thou art in no danger, tell me was it thou who came before to the land of *Fál* to trouble me, thou shining white-toothed, modest-faced lady?

Or art thou she who came afore-time to visit the Round Table, thou head of smooth, fair, bright locks, to wondrous King Arthur?

Or art thou she who came to great *Aodh*, son of *Ughoine*, from the seductive streams of the fairy mound of Slievenamon to the mortal plain of Ireland?

Or art thou she who came another time to the camp of Brian *Bóroimhe*, to bear Murrough across the Irish Sea, and eastwards across the surface of the ocean?

Or art thou she who came from bright, fruitful Rathtrim to beguile the son of *Deichtine*, the valorous Hound of *Culann*?

Or art thou she that came afore-time, thou bright, angel-like form, to the land of battlesome *Banbha*, to *Mathghamhain Ó Máille*?

Or art thou she who came again to seduce the youths, in the days of *Conaire*, O bright cheek, to the chosen host of Teltown?

Or art thou she, thou staunch heart, who bore Bran, son of white-footed *Feabhal*, across the smooth surface of the sea, to the chosen Land of Promise?

There came, perhaps thou art of them, to the King of Connacht – a famous visit, beautiful women – a gathering of power, to the shores of noble Loch Derg.

Or didst thou beguile *Connla* the Red, from the host of *Banbha* of the cold, wet summits; O bright form, not unseemly of looks, though he was guarded by the sages of the people?

Or didst thou beguile myself before, thou shining form, since thou, O slender fairy-like lady, art continually spoiling the men of Ireland?

All the more do I suspect that thou art the other woman I saw, because there is none save thee to equal her in beautiful, leafy *Banbha*.

There is not in the fairy mounds of the Boyne a woman of thy beauty save that woman, nor in the fair castles of *Síodh na gCuan*, thou gentle, white-formed, pleasing one.

Nor in the fairy mound of oared Assaroe, or in the castle of the *Ioldánach*'s fosterfather, or in the smooth, warm-couched mound of Trim, or in the many-shaped castle of *Eochall*.

After her no woman shall we see in dream or in fantasy, until she comes to us again, returning in a vision.

Once or twice has my form been blighted by her soft face, it will happen a third time, the wondrous, shining beauty.

I SHALL NOT DIE
translated by Frank O'Connor

I shall not die because of you
   O woman though you shame the swan,
They were foolish men you killed,
   Do not think me a foolish man.

Why should I leave the world behind
   For the soft hand, the dreaming eye,
The crimson lips, the breasts of snow –
   Is it for these you'd have me die?

Why should I heed the fancy free,
  The joyous air, the eye of blue,
The side like foam, the virgin neck?
  I shall not die because of you.

The devil take the golden hair!
  That maiden look, that voice so gay,
That delicate heel and pillared thigh
  Only some foolish man would slay.

O woman though you shame the swan
  A wise man taught me all he knew,
I know the crooked ways of love,
  I shall not die because of you.

ADVICE TO LOVERS
translated by Frank O'Connor

The way to get on with a girl
Is to drift like a man in a mist,
Happy enough to be caught,
Happy to be dismissed.

Glad to be out of her way,
Glad to rejoin her in bed,
Equally grieved or gay
To learn that she's living or dead.

From MY LIFE AND LOVES
by Frank Harris

It was at Ballinasloe that I was surprised by the sheer loveliness of the innkeeper's daughter. I had been walking and working hard for some time, and was minded to take it easy for a week or so when I came to his inn. The girl captivated me; she hadn't much to do and they liked to hire their jaunting car to me, and I got into the habit of taking Molly (Margaret was her name) with me everywhere as a guide. Her mother had long been dead and the father found enough to do in his bar while her elder sister took charge of the house. So Molly and I spent a good deal of time together: I made up to her from the beginning. Naturally I kissed her as soon as I could and as often as I got the chance and when I told her I loved her, I found she took it much more seriously than I did.

'You wouldn't be after marrying me,' she said; 'you'd be ashamed of me over there in London and Paris and Vienna.' (My boxes showed labels that were known to every one in the house.)

'You're an angel,' I replied, 'but I have a lot to do before I can think of marrying.' Still the kissing and caressing went on continually.

I have not even described Molly, and yet I shall always see her as she stood before me that first night: she was as tall as I was, and splendidly formed, of the mother-type with large breasts and hips; she held her head turned away as if she did not want to see me while I gazed at her; but her flower face was finer even than her figure: the great grey eyes shaded with long black lashes that curled up; while masses of very dark hair fell to her waist. Curiously enough her skin was as fair as that of a blonde; when she turned half smiling, half fearful to me:

'Have you seen enough now?'

I could only give her another kiss and exclaim:

'I could look a long time without ever having enough, you beauty!'

'Sure, I'm like everybody else and my cousin Anne Moriarty's the beauty, with her golden hair!'

'Nothing like so beautiful as you!'

'How do you know, you haven't seen her?'

For answer, I kissed her.

'You'll catch cold, you'll come tomorrow?' She nodded and I went to bed in a fever; I had failed absolutely; but I was in no hurry and ultimate failure was unthinkable.

I got into the habit of taking my dinner in my sitting-room, for there was seldom any one in the public dining-room and when my things were cleared away and I sat reading Molly would come in and we'd talk like lovers. One evening I asked her why she didn't come to my room after every one was asleep.

To my amazement she said she'd love to and I made her promise to come that very night, scarcely daring to believe in my good fortune. About eleven I heard the pattering of bare feet and as I opened the door that gave into my sitting-room, there was Molly with nothing but a red Indian shawl over her nightie. In bed together I kissed and kissed her and she responded, but as soon as I tried to go further she held me off.

'Sure you wouldn't be doing anything like that.'

'You don't care for me much or you wouldn't deny me,' was my retort.

'Indeed I would; you must be good for I love to cuddle you,' and she slipped her arms round me and held me to her till I grew almost crazy with desire. At first I smiled to myself; a few nights of preliminaries and nature would be too strong; but I had reckoned without my host.

Again and again I tried, but the denial was adamant. Molly thrilled and melted under my kissing; but would not consent to what she would have to confess afterwards to the priest.

'Please not; be good now!'

'But why, why?'

The question stung her. . . .

'How could I ever go to Church? I confess every month; sure it's a mortal sin!'

'No sin at all and who'd know?'

'Father Sheridan would ask me; sure, he knows I like you; I told him.'

'And he'd condemn it?'

'Oh my! That's why I can come to you because none of them would even dream that I'd come like this to you – but I love to hold you and hear you talk and to think I please you, makes me so proud and glad – '

'Don't you love my kisses best?'

'They make me afraid. Talk to me now; tell me of all the places you've seen; I've been reading of Paris – it must be lovely – wonderful – and the French girls dress so well – oh, I'd love to travel – '

A few days later, I made it my business to meet Father Sheridan and found him very intelligent; he was of the old school, had been brought up in St Omer and had a delightful French tincture of reading and humour; but alas, he was as crazy as any Irish-bred priest on the necessity of chastity. I drew him out on the subject and found him eloquent; at his fingertips he had all the statistics of illegitimacy and was proud of the fact that it was five times less frequent in Ireland than in England, and to my amusement I found it was commoner in Wales than in Scotland; Sheridan would never admit that the Welsh were Christians at all – 'All Pagans,' he'd say with intense emphasis, 'mere savages without a church or a saint!'

He was proud of the fact, I found, that it was his duty to denounce a young man and woman from the pulpit if they kept company too long, or with a suspicion of undue intimacy.

'They should marry and not burn,' was a favourite phrase of his: 'The children of young parents are always healthy and strong;' it was an obsession with him. Yet he would drink whisky with me till we both had had more than enough.

93

How do the Irish come to have this insane belief in the necessity and virtue of chastity? It is their unquestioned religious belief that gives it them; yet in the mountains of Bavaria and in parts of the Abruzzi the peasants are just as religious, and there too chastity is highly esteemed, but nothing to be compared to its power in Ireland. I have often wondered why.

To cut a long story short I used all the knowledge I had with Molly, yet failed completely, and with failure in the nightly lists, Ballinasloe soon became intolerable to me. I had long ago exhausted all the beauties of the neighbourhood and had come to the conclusion that outside love the place was as devoid of intellectual interest as a town in Western America. The priest I couldn't talk to, the lawyers and doctors were all tenth-rate; some of the younger men were eager to learn and came to the inn in the evening to hear me talk; but – I too had 'to be about my Father's business'. I went for a trip to Londonderry to study the citadel of Irish Protestantism, and to make the final parting with Molly easier. When I returned, I didn't ask her to come to me at night; what was the good? but the night before I went to Belfast she came and I explored with her some of the side-paths of affection, and confessed with all frankness that since I met Smith I was all ambition; under a vow, so to speak, to develop every faculty I had at any cost.

'I am not ambitious, Molly, of place or power or riches; but of knowledge and wisdom I'm the lover and priest, resolved to let nothing stand in the way.'

I explained to her that that was the reason why I had come to Ireland, just as the same desire of knowledge had driven me years before round the world, and would no doubt drive me again.

'I don't want happiness even, Molly, nor comfort, though I'll take all I can get of both; but they're not my aim or purpose; I'm wedded to the one quest like a knight of the Holy Grail and my whole life will go to that achievement. Don't ask me why! I don't know; I only know that Smith, my friend and professor in Lawrence, Kansas, lit the sacred fire in me and I'll go on till death. You must not think I don't care for you: I do with all my heart; you're a great woman, heart and soul and body; but my work calls me and I must go.'

'I've always felt it,' she said quietly, 'always felt that you would not stay here or marry any one here. I understand, and I only hope your ambition may make you happy, for without happiness, without love, is there anything worth having in life? I can't believe it; but then I'm only a girl. If you ever thought of coming back, write first – to see you suddenly would stop my heart with joy....'

From LETTERS TO MOLLY:
John Millington Synge to Maire O'Neill 1906–1909
edited by Ann Saddlemyer

Glendalough Ho.
Wednesday [?25–26 June 1907]

My little Heart's Core

I want you to find this in your little paw when you awake tomorrow morning to drive away your depression. I have had a long talk about you with my mother, and I feel cheered-up some how. She seems to have known a lot of cases like yours Mrs X. and Mrs Z. and Miss Y. and so on and they all got well and lived happily ever afterwards. I think it's only fair that you should have a turn at being ill too, if you were too well you wouldn't be able to sympathize with your poor old Tramp when he gets put up on the shelf. Now be very good and very cheerful and take care of yourself.

My mother – on second thoughts – seemed to think it would be rather improper for me to stay in the same cottage with you and Sally. So enquire about other places near by, when you get there. I shall go up on Friday – if it is fine and stay the one night anyhow and see how it suits me and then I can look round. Now be sure and be happy you'll find your poor little illness will only draw us closer together, and make us realize how much we love each other – if that is possible. (I mean I dont think we'll ever really know how dear we are to each other.)

For ever and ever my own poor darling
Your old Tramp

[30 May 1907]

Dearest

I've started, out through our little tunnel past Killiney Strand past our *little lighthouse* then into Bray and on round the Head where we found the *puppy dog!* How it is all mixed up with you now. I am below Wicklow and the rain has stopped. The country is beautifully green under the clouds. I can hardly write the train is shaking so much. I wonder what I'll do with myself the three hours in Wexford before I sail. I feel lonesome and sad, here all by myself. The half lifted cloud is very beautiful and I'm seeing great sights all the same.

Arklow. My spirits are going UP. The country is wonderful, masses of bluebells, and wet green trees and ferns everywhere. It's wonderful after the long imprisonment I've had. I wonder could *we* come home by

White's Hotel Wexford.
Thursday night

I am in Wexford now as you see trying to pass my evening I have two hours more to get through. I wish I could write to you for two hours I dont know what else I am to do. I have just had tea and plaice at the end of a big table, and there are three men at a table near discussing the world. I thought at first they were commercials but they seem to have too much information and knowledge for that noble calling. One of them has just told a fearsome tale on the effects of hypnotism – or mesmerism as you call it – I'll tell it to you by and by when we meet. Now they are on the Rebellion and they seem to know a lot about it.

It seems funny to me to be on the road again I have been so long shut up. Certainly there is nothing like travelling. I feel better already. It is one of the wettest nights I have ever come across, it is coming down in bucket-fulls so I cant walk about any where. This is like writing when you are hypnotized because I'm scribbling away as hard as I can and all the time I'm listening to the talk at the table behind me. I dont know how much this trip will cost, I like this route it has something out of the common. Did I tell you I am not to get to Jack Yeats' till a quarter past one tomorrow. Isn't that a good trot? By the way I had a funny incident today. You know my old breeches are in bits. 'Well' – as you say – I bought a new pair ready made yesterday to wear on my journey with my old coat and waistcoat I hadn't time to try them on till an hour before I was to start. I put them on then and found them – I thought – mighty elegant. Then I sat down plump, to put on my shoes, and I heard a rend. The seam in the gable end had split right down and there I was! Fancy if that had happened when I was getting into the train after I had started. I dragged them off and got the cook to sew them up as best she could. Now I [am] walking about in great trepidation for fear they'll go again! – I have had a long talk with the waiter, he says they dont half know the bay yet on this line and they have run aground two or three times. I hope we wont be wrecked. If you get this you'll know I'm safe as it's going over with me!

From THE PLAYBOY OF THE WESTERN WORLD, Act III
by J.M.Synge

CHRISTY [*Indignantly*] Starting from you, is it? [*He follows her*] I will not, then, and when the airs is warming, in four months or five, it's then yourself and me should be pacing Neifin in the dews of night, the times sweet smells do be rising, and you'd see a little, shiny new moon, maybe sinking on the hills.

PEGEEN [*Looking at him playfully*] And it's that kind of a poacher's love you'd make, Christy Mahon, on the sides of Neifin, when the night is down?

CHRISTY It's little you'll think if my love's a poacher's, or an earl's itself, when you'll feel my two hands stretched around you, and I squeezing kisses on your puckered lips, till I'd feel a kind of pity for the Lord God is all ages sitting lonesome in His golden chair.

PEGEEN That'll be right fun, Christy Mahon, and any girl would walk her heart out before she'd meet a young man was your like for eloquence, or talk at all.

CHRISTY [*Encouraged*] Let you wait, to hear me talking, till we're astray in Erris, when Good Friday's by, drinking a sup from a well, and making mighty kisses with our wetted mouths, or gaming in a gap of sunshine, with yourself stretched back unto your necklace, in the flowers of the earth.

PEGEEN [*In a low voice, moved by his tone*] I'd be nice so, is it?

CHRISTY [*With rapture*] If the mitred bishops seen you that time, they'd be the like of the holy prophets, I'm thinking, do be straining the bars of paradise to lay eyes on the Lady Helen of Troy, and she abroad, pacing back and forward with a nosegay in her golden shawl.

PEGEEN [*With real tenderness*] And what is it I have, Christy Mahon, to make me fitting entertainment for the like of you, that has such poet's talking, and such bravery of heart?

CHRISTY [*In a low voice*] Isn't there the light of seven heavens in your heart alone, the way you'll be an angel's lamp to me from this out, and I abroad in the darkness, spearing salmons in the Owen or the Carrowmore?

PEGEEN If I was your wife I'd be along with you those nights, Christy Mahon, the way you'd see I was a great hand at coaxing bailiffs, or coining funny nicknames for the stars of night.

CHRISTY You is it? Taking your death in the hailstones, or in the fogs of dawn.

PEGEEN Yourself and me would shelter easy in a narrow bush [*with a qualm of dread*]; but we're only talking, maybe, for this would be a poor, thatched place to hold a fine lad is the like of you.

CHRISTY [*Putting his arm around her*] If I wasn't a good Christian, it's on my naked knees I'd be saying my prayers and paters to every jackstraw you have roofing your head, and every stony pebble is paving the laneway to your door.

PEGEEN [*Radiantly*] If that's the truth I'll be burning candles from this out to the miracles of God that have brought you from the south to-day and I with my gowns bought ready, the way that I can wed you, and not wait at all.

CHRISTY It's miracles, and that's the truth. Me there toiling a long while and walking a long while, not knowing at all I was drawing all times nearer to this holy day.

PEGEEN And myself, a girl, was tempted often to go sailing the seas till I'd marry a Jew-man, with ten kegs of gold, and I not knowing at all there was the like of you drawing nearer, like the stars of God.

CHRISTY And to think I'm long years hearing women talking that talk to all bloody fools, and this the first time I've heard the like of your voice talking sweetly for my own delight.

PEGEEN And to think it's me is talking sweetly, Christy Mahon, and I the fright of seven townlands for my biting tongue. Well, the heart's a wonder; and I'm thinking there won't be our like in Mayo, for gallant lovers, from this hour today.

From GO AWAY, OLD MAN, GO AWAY
by Patrick Boyle

'Motherajaysus, are ye still in her bed?' he roared. She came out of the room and stopped in the doorway, yawning and scratching her head – a fine strapping piece, bubbed and bottomed like a tinker woman, with oily jet-black hair, thick sensual lips and dark eyes, blurred and heavy with sleep. The dirty woollen-jumper, sweat-stained at the armpits, barely reached the rumpled partly-fastened skirt. Her bare legs were brown-blotched with the heat of the fire.

She yawned again and knuckled her eyes.

'I just threw myself on the bed a minute,' she said. 'Till the kettle would come to the boil.'

Speechless, he swung aloft the steaming kettle, as if he were exorcizing her with a smoking thurible.

She stared at him open-mouthed.

'What are you aiming to do with that thing?' she demanded.

She darted across the room.

'Give it here, man,' she said, trying to snatch the kettle from him.

He pushed her away roughly.

'Lookat here,' he said dramatically, tilting up the kettle over the hearth so that the few remaining drops went sizzling into the fire. 'Boiled to nothing.'

The sleep had gone out of her eyes: the listlessness from her body. Her sallow face was flushed and her thick lips pouted aggressively. But though her features were distorted with rage, there was about her a curious air of satisfaction as though the very volume of her emotion brought with it some measure of bodily fulfilment.

'Is it trying to quench the fire you are?' she asked.

'Quench be damned. Wouldn't a good spit smother it?'

'Maybe if you had the trouble of lighting it, you wouldn't be so quick – '

She broke off and, stooping, commenced heaping up the glowing embers with the tongs.

'Listen here, me young tit,' he said, addressing the swaying rump-filled skirt. 'It would fit you better if you stopped home at nights instead of roaming the country. You'll have the priest naming you yet from the altar.'

The strip of white flesh below her rucked-up jumper, winking at every movement, kept ogling at him slyly.

'A man at my time of life slaving and sweating like a Turk while his wife goes trapeezing around the country to every bit of a dance or a card game that's held in the parish. Sure I must be the laughing stock of half-Europe.'

His gaze travelled down to the creased hollows behind her knees.

'Letting a man off to his work without a bite to eat. Have you no shame in you?'

He moistened his flabby craving lips.

'The women ... they're a terror ... the same the world over ... rising a mutiny wherever they be ...'

He pushed out a tentative hand, but at once let it fall to his side and remained staring at her dumbly, his eyes sick and glazed with desire.

Across her shoulder she looked – taunting him with bold mocking eyes.

'Give over,' she said. 'It's the same ould tune – day in, day out. It's a wonder you took me at all, the way you go on.'

The old man struggled for speech.

'Ye–Ye–Ye–Ye're damned smart, aren't ye.'

Failing to think of any more crushing remark, he spat viciously into the heart of the fire and turned away. At the door he shouted back:

'And don't be the whole day getting me me bloody bit of breakfast.'

Outside, he squatted on the low window-sill – tired, hungry, emotionally deflated.

You common idiot, he told himself. Letting that one get the better of you with a few flirts of her backside and her stooping over the fire to give you a right view of her where-withal. As if it wasn't sticking out like the side of a church at the best of times. Up half the night jack-acting and then basking the day long in her bed, snoring and grunting like a sow at the pigging. And across in the bog making slaughter of himself is no less a person than the boss of the house – the boss; how are you! – hugging his grinding puddings with sheer starvation. The impudent trollop, slooching around half-dressed, the bare ones scalded off her with the heat of the fire and the two elders swinging out of her like she was six months gone. God above, man, I don't know what you see in her.

DO YOU REMEMBER THAT NIGHT?
translated by Eugene O'Curry

Do you remember that night
When you were at the window
With neither hat nor gloves
Nor coat to shelter you?

I reached out my hand to you
And you ardently grasped it,
I remained to converse with you
Until the lark began to sing.

Do you remember that night
That you and I were
At the foot of the rowan tree
And the night drifting snow?
Your head on my breast,
And your pipe sweetly playing?
Little thought I that night
That our love ties would loosen!

Beloved of my inmost heart,
Come some night, and soon,
When my people are at rest,
That we may talk together.
My arms shall encircle you
While I relate my sad tale,
That your soft, pleasant converse
Hath deprived me of heaven.

The fire is unraked,
The light unextinguished,
The key under the door,
Do you softly draw it.
My mother is asleep,
But I am wide awake;
My fortune in my hand,
I am ready to go with you.

From THE DIARY OF HUMPHREY O'SULLIVAN
translated by Rev. Michael McGrath SJ

[Humphrey O'Sullivan was born in or near Killarney in
1780 where his father was a schoolteacher. The family
settled in Callan, Co. Kilkenny in 1790. He appears to
have later acquired a draper's shop through marriage to a
Mary Delahunty. His main occupation however was that
of schoolteacher. Humphrey's wife died in 1829.
Humphrey died in 1837. The original diary was written
in Irish.]

The eighteenth day, Wednesday. A sunny cheerful morning
free from fog: midday, with merry sweetvoiced Maggie
Barr and another, I went to Desart, by the same roads which
I took on Easter Sunday. We walked through dark evergreen
pinewoods through fine laneways, now crooked, now
straight, shaded from the face of the sun, listening to the flut-
ing of the lark in the wayside meadows, to the delicate note
of the blackbird, male and female, of the thrush, and of every
other sweetvoiced bird, in unison with soft sweet liquid-
voiced Maggie Barr. We lost our way in a dark mysterious
dell, so that we could no longer tell east or west, north or
south. At long last we came through mossy hollows, through
brakes of briar, glens of ash, groves of evergreen pine to a
glade of puddles, pools and loughlets, of rivulets, waterfalls
and chattering (of birds and streams). Here were the white
duck and the dappled drake, the blackbird high on the top
of the hawthorns, greeting one another.
  'I'm tired,' said soft, sweet, liquid-voiced Maggie.
  'So am I,' said I. 'Let us sit awhile on the moss on the rock.'
  'Let us, by all means.'
  What with the murmur of the waterfalls, soft-voiced
Maggie slumbered.
  'Move, thou wind, with thy softest crooning through the
trees of the swamp. Be not loudvoiced nor blustering!'

The wind blew gently through the weary wanderer's hair, laying bare a neck as white as swan on pool. Her tiny lips were red as rowan berries and sweet as honey, her white breasts like twin snowclad mountainets rising and falling like the waves of the King's River, her slim little waist, her tidy seat, her pretty legs hidden by her satin gown even to her shapely feet. Suddenly two snipe darted, from a swamp close by, through the air as an arrow from a bow. The beauteous maiden started from her sound sleep.

'May there never be a pool for you in Ireland henceforth and for ever!'

'May there never be a one! The sun is sinking towards the west. Let us move on homewards.'

We ended our way faint and weary, her arm in mine, her head on my shoulder, her eyes bent on the ground. I do not recall a happier day ...

THE MAID THAT SOLD HER BARLEY
traditional ballad

It's cold and raw the northwinds blow
Black in the morning early,
When all the hills were covered with snow,
Oh then it was winter fairly.
As I was riding o'er the moor,
I met a farmer's daughter,
Her cherry cheeks and sloe black eyes,
They caused my heart to falter.

I bowed my bonnet very low
To let her know my meaning.
She answered with a courteous smile,
Her looks they were engaging.
'Where are you bound my pretty maid,
It's now in the morning early,'
The answer that she made to me,
'Kind sir, to sell my barley.'

'Now twenty guineas I've in my purse,
And twenty more that's yearly,
You need not go to the market town,
For I'll buy all your barley.
If twenty guineas would gain the heart,
Of the maid that I love so dearly,
All for to tarry with me one night,
And go home in the morning early.'

As I was riding o'er the moor
The very evening after,
It was my fortune for to meet
The farmer's only daughter.
Although the weather being cold and raw
With her I thought to parley,
This answer then she made to me,
'Kind sir, I've sold my barley.'

THE BROW OF NEFIN
translated by Douglas Hyde

Did I stand on the bald top of Néfin
  And my hundred-times loved one with me,
We should nestle together as safe in
  Its shade as the birds on a tree.

From your lips such a music is shaken
    When you speak it awakens my pain,
And my eyelids by sleep are forsaken
    And I seek for my slumber in vain.

But were I on the fields of the ocean,
    I should sport on its infinite room,
I should plough through the billow's commotion
    Though my friends should look dark at my doom.
For the flower of all maidens of magic
    Is beside me where'er I may be,
And my heart like a coal is extinguished,
    Not a woman takes pity on me.

How well for the birds in all weather,
    They rise up on high in the air
And then sleep upon one bough together
    Without sorrow or trouble or care;
But so it is not in this world
    For myself and my thousand-times fair,
For away, far apart from each other,
    Each day rises barren and bare.

Say, what dost thou think of the heavens
    When the heat overmasters the day,
Or what when the steam of the tide
    Rises up in the face of the bay?
Even so is the man who has given
    An inordinate love-gift away,
Like a tree on a mountain all riven
    Without blossom or leaflet or spray.

THE THORNY CLIFF
traditional folk-song

One morning as I roved out by the outskirts of the woods
I was stricken by an arrow, and no cure could be found for
   me.
I beheld a sportive maiden beneath a thorny cliff.
My heart within leaped high for joy – and no cure could be
   found for me.

Alas, that I am not a mavis,
Through the laneway would I deftly steal,
And my strain would I sing for you till the day would
   brightly dawn.
If I came across a wise old woman who owned a cow or sheep
I should drive it to the fair with her and have amusement
   thereby.

The women-topers wail aloud –
Jesus, Son, give them no help.
When the purse is empty, and my heart within is grieved,
My hope is yet to find her – alas, I never shall.
And it's like a dart from a wedge or iron – is not love a
   wasting ill?

My love is adown the garden – a hound, a deer, a steed,
She's a fairer captive than man e'er laid eyes upon.
Though tall be the elder, and fall its blossoms low,
No dew lies in the desert, and there's darkness in the sun.

I shall hie me off to Egypt, or some island hard by;
Or to America shall I go at eve of summer with my first love,
   if I live.
Back till doom I will not come – till the cuckoo calls in
   winter,
And till the castle which the Milesians built is being raised
   again anew.

My friends are on all sides of me – no converse can I hold.
There's hard strict watch kept over me if I go out at night.
Do not tie up my fingers – leave them prepared.
My suit of clothes, my coffin – I will not ask a shroud.

THE POET LOVES FROM AFAR
translated by Desmond O'Grady

I think I shall live for a while a bit gamely
And stop making out to be what I'm not;
The strong minded women who turn men tamely
Without a doubt are a dangerous lot.

Although it's the women of beauty and stature
That unmarried men most want to wed;
A girl called Grainne – the girl I'm after –
Is the woman I'd like to take to my bed.

If I had the choice and the pick of all women;
The finest in Ireland, in Scotland and France;
I'd like nothing more than a night's wild loving
With that young one I saw at the crossroads dance.

Cross-roads dancing and the pursuits of peace time were not
for Robert Emmet, one of Ireland's patriots. As a young
man he proved that he was a stoic. He once swallowed

poison by mistake and, rather than waken his father who was a doctor, he looked up the encyclopedia to find out what was the prophylactic. His love had something of the same reserve. His sweetheart was eighteen-year-old Sarah Curran and their story is regarded as a personal loss for love and a personal loss for Ireland. The rebellion he led was foiled, and in true Irish fashion he was betrayed by one of his own men. Early one morning he was hanged at Kilmainham Gaol, then he was grasped by the hair and dragged around and they say the dogs came to lick his blood. One person from the Highland Regiment dipped his handkerchief in it and thrust it to his bosom. In a carriage stationed a short distance from the scene was Sarah with her face buried in a handkerchief. This is how her love has been described:

From THE UNITED IRISHMEN:
Their Life and Times
by R. R. Madden

She loved him with the disinterested fervour of a woman's first and early love. When every worldly maxim arrayed itself against him, when blasted in fortune, and disgrace and danger darkened around his name, she loved him the more ardently for his very sufferings. If, then, his fate could awaken the sympathy even of his foes, what must have been the agony of her whose soul was occupied with his image? Let those tell who have had the portals of the tomb suddenly closed between them and the being they most loved on earth – who have sat at its threshold, as one shut out in a cold and lonely world, from whence all that was most lovely and loving had departed.

To render her widowed situation more desolate, she had incurred her father's displeasure by her unfortunate attachment, and was an exile from her parental roof. But could the sympathy and offices of friends have reached a spirit so shocked and *driven in* by horror, she would have experienced no want of consolation; for the Irish are proverbially a people of quick and generous sensibilities. The most delicate and cherishing attentions were paid her by families of wealth and distinction. She was led into society, and they tried by all kinds of occupation and amusement to dissipate her grief, and wean her from the tragic story of her love. But it was all in vain. There are some strokes of calamity, that scathe and scorch the soul – that penetrate to the vital seat of happiness – and blast it, never again to put forth bud or blossom. She never objected to frequent the haunts of pleasure, but she was as much alone there as in the depths of solitude. She walked about in a sad reverie, apparently unconscious of the world around her. She carried with her an inward woe, that mocked at all the blandishments of friendship, and 'heeded not the song of the charmer, charm he never so wisely'.

On the occasion of a masquerade at the Rotunda, her friends brought her to it. There can be no exhibition of far-gone wretchedness more striking and painful, than to meet it in such a scene. To find it wandering, like a spectre, lonely and joyless, where all around is gay – to see it dressed out in the trappings of mirth, and looking so wan and woe-begone, as if it had tried in vain to cheat the poor heart into a momentary forgetfulness of sorrow. After strolling through the splendid rooms, and giddy crowd, with an air of abstraction, she sat down on the steps of an orchestra, and looking about for some time with a vacant air, that shewed insensibility to the gayish scene, she began, with the capriciousness of a sickly heart, to warble a little plaintive air. She had an exquisite voice; but, on this occasion, it was so simple, so touching, it breathed forth such a soul of wretchedness, that she gathered a crowd, mute and silent, around her, and melted every one into tears.

Parnell was not pitied for unrequited love. In fact he incurred the wrath of the Irish and precipitated his political downfall because he chose to love a married woman, Katherine O'Shea. As he embarked on it he knew that it would be to his detriment.

'There will be a howl,' he said, and thought of those Irish fools who believed that form and creed can govern men and life. He wrote to Mrs O'Shea on 6 November saying how disappointed he was that he had not received a letter from her or her husband. The very next letter contains the key to her house which he took by mistake. From then on it is 'Darling' and 'Wifie' and 'Queenie' and 'My own gem'.

From CHARLES STEWART PARNELL
by Katherine O'Shea

Dublin
Wednesday night, November 11, 1880

My Dearest Love, – I have made all arrangements to be in London on Saturday morning, and shall call at Keppel Street for a letter from you. It is quite impossible for me to tell you just how very much you have changed my life, what a small interest I take in what is going on about me, and how I detest everything which has happened during the last few days to keep me away from you – I think of you always, and you must never believe there is to be any 'fading'. By the way, you must not send me any more artificial letters. I want as much of your own self as you can transfer into written words, or else none at all. – Yours always,

C.S.P.

A telegram goes to you, and one to W.* tomorrow, which are by no means strictly accurate.

November 21, 1881

My Own Queenie, – Yours of the 18th has reached me safely, and though I am relieved to know that my darling is a little less miserable, yet I am still very much troubled and anxious about you. Has he [Captain O'Shea] left yet? It is frightful that you should be exposed to such daily torture. My own Wifie must try and strengthen herself and get some sleep for her husband's sake and for our child's sake, who must be suffering much also. . . .

[The baby died but the world believed it was Captain O'Shea's.]

* Captain O'Shea.

LETTER FROM JONATHAN SWIFT TO VANESSA

Addressed: To Mrs Van-Homrigh, at Mr
Handcock's in Little Rider Street,
near St James's Street, London.

Postmark: Wantage, 13 Au.

Endorsed: 6

August 12th, 1714

I had your letter last post, and before you can send me another
I shall set out for Ireland. I must go and take the oaths, and
the sooner the better. I think, since I have known you, I have
drawn an old house upon my head. You should not have
come by Wantage for a thousand pound. You used to brag
you were very discreet. Where is it gone? It is probable I
may not stay in Ireland long, but be back by the beginning
of winter. When I am there, I will write to you as soon as
I can conveniently, but it shall be always under a cover; and
if you write to me, let some other direct it; and I beg you
will write nothing that is particular, but which may be seen;
for I apprehend letters will be opened and inconveniences
will happen. If you are in Ireland while I am there I shall
see you very seldom. It is not a place for any freedom, but
where ever[y]thing is known in a week and magnified a
hundred degrees. These are rigorous laws that must be passed
through; but it is probable we may meet in London in
winter, or if not, leave all to Fate, that seldom cares to
humour our inclinations. I say all this out of the perfect
esteem and friendship I have for you. These public mis-
fortunes have altered all my measures and broke my spirits.
God almighty bless you. I shall, I hope, be on horseback in
a day after this comes to your hand. I would not answer your
questions for a million, nor can I think of them with any ease
of mind. Adieu.

She did of course follow him as did Mrs Johnson (Stella). Stella may have been the quieter of the two but she was also the victorious. She wrote to Swift to remind him that she had forsaken her country and clouded her reputation and was not insensible to his recent indifference. She did not mention Vanessa, but she broached marriage. He would go through with it to ease her mind but it must be a secret and they must live separately and guardedly, as before. Vanessa had retired to Celbridge to seclusion and despair. As his letters came her passion increased and lonelier she became. She took up the cudgels and wrote to Stella. Stella informed her of their marriage and sent Swift Vanessa's accusatory letter. In a paroxysm Swift rode on horseback to Vanessa's house, flung the envelope on the table and instantly left. When Vanessa died a few weeks later Swift's mind became so dreadful and so agitated that he had to repair to the South, and there in rage and grief exorcize his guilt.

From INISHFALLEN, FARE THEE WELL
by Sean O'Casey

Nora wasn't for him: she would forever shelter in the lee of a credulous respectability. He remembered well, once, when she was telling him she'd have to cease from seeing him, how savagely she had declared that if he failed to make a name for himself in what he was trying to do within six months, their sweet alliance must end forever. He remembered how resentfully his soul laughed at the threat, for his development was with life, and not with calendar or clock. The Holy Ghost was not a panting creature of time, yet here was a good catholic girl trying to goad him into a hurry. The Holy Ghost in a hurry! She was measuring the gay-coloured wings of the Holy Ghost, hiding eternity with their spread, with the pale wings, stable as dust, of the frail, flying moth of time. There were other months in the year as well as May in which to go gathering nuts.

Let her cling to the little house, with its tiny windows and door; its four small rooms, with their neat little beds; the windows graced with curtains. They were her due, and she did well to claim them for her own. They were genuine things, to be sought after by the sensible and satisfied. The lions had long departed from the Christians. Sean didn't despise them, either; he wished he could dwell in one of them, in peace, secure as this world goes; with freedom to go, if ever one of these tiny, gentle things tried to enwrap his soul with lies. But he would be safer, if need be, walking the roads, or crouching, like blind Rafferty, under a dripping bush, while the rain fell and the wind blew keen. Not for Nora the charm of embroidered cloths under her feet, but the firmness of well-glazed oilcloth, or the softness of a carpet, well woven, covering a floor. Not the red rose, with its agitating thorn, for her swan-white breast, but a black cross, nestling chill and steady there.

Never once had he mentioned the Bolshevik Revolution to her, though it was ever in his mind; never once had he tried by a word to attune her ear to an echo even of the march of the Red Guards, though he himself had followed, with quaking heart, the advance of Kolchak from the east, and the advance of Denikin from the south, till from where they were, Denikin said, they could see, on a clear night, through the windows of Moscow, the tight-lipped people getting ready to quit the city. The Press was full of the death and defeat of the Red madmen; then, suddenly they fell silent; and Sean knew that the Red Flag was high in Moscow and Petrograd. O, silver trumpets be ye lifted up, and call to the great race that is to come! Yeats, Yeats, they are sounding now, though your ears are cocked in another direction. Sounding loud and brave, not for all ears yet; but for the many to hear; and

Sean's were the first of the Irish ones to hear them. Christ the king was becoming a Communist!

He knew in his heart that Nora and he would never fix themselves together in the world. Freethought to her would be but blasphemy and ruin eternal. A big part of her life would become a mumble of prayer that he might recognise the truth, accept the faith, be converted, and live. Jesus! that would be death in life to him! After the first while or so, her creed would again form her life, and then his crowded loneliness would end forever. Let her gentle, quiet nature live a quiet, gentle life; let his doubting, strenuous one live out its activity and struggle, however bitter and painful, any, or all, of it might be.

He stood still to watch the tired and shallow flow of the slow waters of the Dodder, near Rathfarnham; hard set at times to push a way through the thick and sturdy herbage, growing querulously far out from its banks, shoving a passage often to the centre of the river; so like the flow of Ireland's life. Above him, the evening had pulled a curtain over the sky of quiet rose and daring green, now patterned with the shapes of hundreds of deep-black rooks, like darkened souls flying off, half afraid of heaven; while in the east, a pale moon, shy and pearly, stole into sight like a shy lass stealing out to meet a wild lover alone for the first time in her life. And around in the sheltering herbage he saw dim forms of life commingling, each a lover and his lass embedded in all the loveliness surrounding them.

> You say there is no substance here,
> One great reality above;
> Back from that void I shrink in fear,
> And, child-like, hide myself in love;
> Show me what angels feel. Till then,
> I cling, a mere weak man, to men.

He felt that he could never be alone, however lonely he might be.

A LULLABY
by Eoghan Rua Ó Súilleabháin,
translated by Padraig O Broin

Though I have been handy with lips and with speech,
  At making verses and spending my own,
I was gulled by a heartless girl till I took
  A baby to nurse – and I dry as a stone.

When first I saw that lovely young maid
  – Her eyes that were blue and the head shyly bent –
And she did not withdraw when I moved to her side,
  Little I knew the affliction she meant.

Her eyes full of mischief, ready and willing –
  Loveliness playing love's dream in the grass.
Yet she was the one left me in this fix
  Dandling a child with a larynx of brass.

From MAKE STRAIGHT FOR THE SHORE
by Benedict Kiely

She taught me to make beds. She taught me to mitre sheets
as neatly as any young nurse ever did in any hospital. She
taught me as the woman lovely in her bones taught the poet:
Turn and Counter-turn and Touch and Stand. The outlaw bull,
benevolent, beneficent in his secret Castledawson meadow,
bellowed his blessing: and I taught her a lot about King Charles
and Robert Burns. Not the Charles who lost his head,
I assured her, but the Charles who held on to his head and
had all the women he could count. Like Rudolf Valentino.

– The blackguard.

– Who?

– Both of them. Easy for him and he a king.

– Valentino wasn't a king.

– He was a film-star.

– He died from sleeping with women.

That was a gentlemanly way of putting what we then happily and enviously believed.

– He should have slept on his own, so.

But it wasn't often that we argued seriously. King Charles on the run from the Roundheads and the lass, who, according to the legend and the poem that Robert Burns based on the legend, made the bed for the fugitive king were better company for us than Valentino who had it all too easy: I bow'd fu' low unto this maid, And thank'd her for her courtesie; I bow'd fu' low unto this maid, and bade her mak a bed to me. . . .

Loftily, and with the style of a man who was a scholar when he hadn't better things to occupy his mind, I told her: Some people say that it wasn't about King Charles at all but Robbie Burns writing about himself and remembering some girl he met in some inn. He met a lot of girls and wrote a lot of poems about them.

– He was a bit of a playboy, she said. My uncle who's a teacher near Limavady knows a lot about Burns. He was standing in a gateway with a girl, Burns was . . .

She was turning the upper sheet, patting down pillows.

. . . and a wee fellow came by. Eating a bun. And stopped to look. And Robert there and then made a poem: Walk on my son and munch your bun. The works of nature maun be done.

In our places Burns was as much part of the folklore as he was in the land he was born in.

We laughed over the story. We tackled the bed in the next room. Once only had I to run and hide when a stout, supervising, old lady came along. Trudi, while I stood mute in a built-in wardrobe, sang, sweetly and with a Scots accent as good as real, that her love was like a red red rose. In the darkness I thought: She took her mither's holland sheets, and made them a' in sarks to me. Blyth and merry may she be, the lass that made the bed to me.

Burns and the lass and the king, perhaps, were with us in whatever room we happened to be in. They didn't intrude. They encouraged us in happiness and folly. Long afterwards I read a translation from some Spanish (I think) poet, and knew then what we were up to and, because I couldn't put it better myself, memorised the words: My chosen part to be with a girl and alone with her secret and her gift.

ON THE DEATH OF HIS WIFE
by Muireadach O'Dalaigh, translated by Frank O'Connor

I parted from my life last night,
    A woman's body sunk in clay:
The tender bosom that I loved
    Wrapped in a sheet they took away.

The heavy blossom that had lit
    The ancient boughs is tossed and blown;
Hers was the burden of delight
    That long had weighed the old tree down.

And I am left alone tonight
    And desolate is the world I see
For lovely was that woman's weight
    That even last night had lain on me.

Weeping I look upon the place
  Where she used to rest her head –
For yesterday her body's length
  Reposed upon you too, my bed.

Yesterday that smiling face
  Upon one side of you was laid
That could match the hazel bloom
  In its dark delicate sweet shade.

Maelva of the shadowy brows
  Was the mead-cask at my side;
Fairest of all flowers that grow
  Was the beauty that has died.

My body's self deserts me now,
  The half of me that was her own,
Since all I knew of brightness died
  Half of me lingers, half is gone.

The face that was like hawthorn bloom
  Was my right foot and my right side;
And my right hand and my right eye
  Were no more mine than hers who died.

Poor is the share of me that's left
  Since half of me died with my wife;
I shudder at the words I speak;
  Dear God, that girl was half my life.

And our first look was her first love;
  No man had fondled ere I came
The little breasts so small and firm
  And the long body like a flame.

For twenty years we shared a home,
  Our converse milder with each year;

Eleven children in its time
  Did that tall stately body bear.

It was the King of hosts and roads
  Who snatched her from me in her prime:
Little she wished to leave alone
  The man she loved before her time.

Now King of churches and of bells,
  Though never raised to pledge a lie
That woman's hand – can it be true? –
  No more beneath my head will lie.

From THE JOURNAL TO ELIZA
by Laurence Sterne

June 4

Hussy! I have employ'd a full hour upon your sweet sentimental Picture and a couple of hours upon yourself, and with as much kind friendship, as the hour You left me. I deny it: Time lessens no Affections which honour and merit have planted. I would give more, and hazard more now for your happiness than in any one period, since I first learn'd to esteem you. Is it so with thee, my friend? has absence weaken'd my Interest, has time worn out any Impression, or is Yorick's name less Musical in Eliza's ears? My heart smites me, for asking the question. 'Tis Treason against thee, Eliza, and Truth – Ye are dear Sisters, and your Brother Bramin Can never live to see a Separation amongst Us. What a similitude in our Trials whilst asunder! Providence has order'd every Step better, than we could have order'd them, for the particular good we wish each other. This you will comment upon and find the *Sense of* without my explanation.

I wish this Summer and Winter with all I am to go through with in them, in business and Labour and Sorrow, well over. I have much to compose and much to dis-compose me; have my Wife's projects and my own Views arising out of them, to harmonize and turn to account; I have Millions of heart aches to suffer and reason with – and in all this Storm of Passions, I have but one small Anchor, Eliza! to keep this weak Vessel of mine from perishing. I trust all I have to it, as I trust Heaven, which cannot leave me, without a fault, to perish. May the same just Heaven, my Eliza, be that eternal Canopy which shall shelter thy head from evil *till we* meet. Adieu, adieu, adieu.

LETTER FROM GEORGE BERNARD SHAW
TO CHARLOTTE PAYNE-TOWNSHEND

29 Fitzroy Square W
13th July 1897

I have an iron ring around my chest, which tightens and grips my heart when I remember that you are perhaps still tormented. Loosen it, oh ever dear to me, by a word to say that you slept well and have never been better than today. Or else lend me my fare to Australia, to Siberia, to the mountains of the moon, to any place where I can torment nobody but myself. I am sorry – not vainly sorry; for I have done a good morning's work, but painfully, wistfully, affectionately sorry that you were hurt; but if you had seen my mind you would not have been hurt. I am so certain of that, that I am in violently, brutally high spirits in spite of that iron ring. Write me something happy, but only a few words; and don't sit down to *think* over them. What you think is all wrong.

GBS

P.S. I am going out to lunch & to Grant Richard's shop. If you send a line between, say, 4 & 5.30 (after which I think I will go off for a thousand leagues on the bike) I shall be here to receive it. Oh, the ring, the ring: hasten to ease it a little: it clutched me bitterly just then.

LETTER FROM GEORGE BERNARD SHAW TO ELLEN TERRY

> The midnight train – gets to Dorking
> at 1 (a.m.) 14–15th June 1897 –
> stopping just now, but will joggle like
> mad presently

Do you read these jogged scrawls, I wonder. I think of your poor eyes, and resolve to tear what I have written up: then I look out at the ghostly country and the beautiful night, and I cannot bring myself to read a miserable book: I *must* talk to you: nowhere else, no time else, can we be so perfectly alone. Yes, as you guess, Ellen, I am having a bad attack of you just at present. I am restless; and a man's restlessness always means a woman; and my restlessness means Ellen. And your conduct is often shocking. Today I was wandering somewhere, thinking busily about what I supposed to be high human concerns when I glanced at a shop window; and there you were – oh disgraceful and abandoned – in your 3rd Act Sans Gene dress – a mere waistband – laughing wickedly, and saying maliciously: 'Look here: restless one, at your pillow, at what you are really thinking about.' How can you look Window & Grove's camera in the face with such thoughts in your head and almost nothing on. You are worse than Lilith, Adam's first wife.

Oh fie, fie, let me get away from this stuff, which you have been listening to all your life, & despise – though indeed, dearest Ellen, these silly longings stir up great waves of tenderness in which there is no guile. You were right about my letters: only it is not boredom, but exhaustion. That is the worst of letters: I must say something: I can't in pen and ink rest these bruised brains in your lap & unburden my heart with inarticulate cries. When I can think, when I can write, then my ideas fly like stones: you can never be sure that one of them will not hurt you – my very love gets knit into an infernal intellectual fabric that wounds when I mean it to caress; and when I am tired and foolish I am flat & apparently bored. Sometimes that happens to my articles; and then I am terrified, indeed, and must work fiercely to remedy it. When *you* complain, I am terrified another way, thinking that the end has come – for I have only one thing to say to you, and it must get tedious sooner or later. I am particularly tedious at present in this midnight solitary journey, wanting to sleep, and yet to sleep with you. Only, do you know what the consequences would be? Well, about tomorrow at noon when the sun would be warm & the birds in full song, you would feel an irresistible impulse to fly into the woods. And there, to your great astonishment & scandal, you would be *confined* of a baby that would immediately spread a pair of wings and fly, and before you could rise to catch it it would be followed by another & another and another – hundreds of them, and they would finally catch you up & fly away with you to some heavenly country where they would grow into strong sweetheart sons with whom, in defiance of the prayerbook, you would found a divine race. Would you not like to be the mother of your own grandchildren? If you were my mother, I am sure I should carry you away to the tribe in Central America where – but I have a lot of things to say & we are at Redhill already.

I shall find a letter from you when I get back to Lotus, shall I not? Reigate we are at now; and it's a quarter to one. In ten minutes, Dorking station; in seventeen minutes thereafter, Lotus, and a letter. *Only* a letter, perhaps not even that. O Ellen, what will you say when the Recording Angel asks you why none of your sins have my name to them?

What no letter! not even this morning. Oh very good, madam, *ve*-ry good. Sorry I troubled you, I'm sure. Busy these times, no doubt. Of course: don't mention it. Where are my vestry papers? Nothing like prosaic local work – yes: I'll do an interview with 'The St Pancras Londoner' about the dust destructor and the contractor system. After all, it is in the morning that one had one's wits about one – at night, fatigue & late hours & joggling trains upset a man and make him drivel. Still, there is such a thing as common politeness; and to leave most important letters from a vestryman un-answered, unnoticed – well, no matter.

GBS

THE GERALDINE'S DAUGHTER
by Egan O'Rahilly

O Pearl without darkness, who hast led me into sorrow,
   Listen to me without anger, whilst I tell my story;
Seeing that thou hast keenly shot shafts and darts
   Through my wounds in showers, which have ruined me,
            without strength;
In sooth I would go to Egypt across the sea,
   And to Erin I would never willingly return;
On the strong sea, on land, in bonds, and in joy,
   I would not grieve at being near thee by a river's side with-
       out disturbance.

Branching, plaited, in long folds, in clusters,
   Brightly shining, and limber, are her locks like gold;
Pearls her eyes, as the star of the morning;
   Right slender her eyebrow as a pen-line in form;
The beauteous appearance of her cheek, lime-white as the
          snow,
   Struggling gaily through the effulgence of the rose,
Which caused Phoebus to rush to behold thee above all
          maidens,
   While his forehead was aflame through love for thy
      beauty.

127

White her breasts, as swans beside the sea-shore;
  Her lime-bright, snow-white body of beauty like the sea-
        gull;
Her goodness cannot be all put on parchment;
  The fair mild lily and gentle flower of virgins.
Bright red are her lips, her white teeth without a blemish,
  Which would save from disease thousands such as I;
The noble speech of her tongue learned in histories,
  Brought stout bucks over mountains by the sweetness of
        her voice.

A Phoenix of the Geraldine blood, Grecians of the coast,
  The mild cousin of the children of Milesius of the hosts;
Heroes crushed without mercy by the English,
  Without strength, without land, without princely man-
        sion, without wealth.
In sooth the blood of the Powers and the Barrys,
  And the strong heroes of Bunratty has been twice strained
        through thee;
There is no noble chieftain or warrior of the stock of the
        children of Cashel,
  Who is not akin to the mild faultless maiden.

I know not her peer in Erin or in England,
  In wisdom, in personal charms, in mind, in form;
The accomplished maiden surpassing in virtue and fame
  Helen, through whom thousands perished in the fight;
There is no man living, who would look at morning
  On her face without sorrow, whose grief she would not
        dispel;
O my bondage! O my hardship! I cannot avoid her
  In my slumbers, in my dreams, by night, or by day.

THE PRETTY DAIRY-MAID
translated by James Clarence Mangan

I have loved you, oh mildest and fairest,
    With love that could scarce be more warm –
I have loved you, oh brightest and rarest,
    Not less for your mind than your form.
I've adored you since ever I met you,
    O, Rose without briar or stain,
And if e'er I forsake or forget you
    Let Love be ne'er trusted again.

From AUTOBIOGRAPHY
by W. B. Yeats

I was tortured by sexual desire and had been for many years.
I have often said to myself that some day I would put it all
down in a book that some young man of talent might not
think as I did that my shame was mine alone. It began when
I was fifteen years old. I had been bathing, and lay down in
the sun on the sand on the Third Rosses and covered my
body with sand. Presently the weight of the sand began to
affect the organ of sex, though at first I did not know what
the strange, growing sensation was. It was only at the orgasm
that I knew, remembering some boy's description or the description in my grandfather's encyclopedia. It was many days
before I discovered how to renew that wonderful sensation.
From that on it was a continual struggle against an experience
that almost invariably left me with exhausted nerves. Normal
sexual intercourse does not affect me more than other men,
but that, though never frequent, was plain ruin. It filled me

with loathing of myself; and yet at first pride and perhaps, a little, lack of obvious opportunity, and now love kept me in unctuous celibacy. When I returned to London in my twenty-seventh year I think my love seemed almost hopeless, and I knew that my friends had all mistresses of one kind or another and that most, at need, went home with harlots. Henley, indeed, mocked at any other life. I had never since childhood kissed a woman's lips. At Hammersmith I saw a woman of the town walking up and down in the empty railway station. I thought of offering myself to her, but the old thought came back, 'No, I love the most beautiful woman in the world.'

HER PRAISE
by W. B. Yeats

She is foremost of those that I would hear praised.
I have gone about the house, gone up and down
As a man does who has published a new book,
Or a young girl dressed out in her new gown,
And though I have turned the talk by hook or crook
Until her praise should be the uppermost theme,
A woman spoke of some new tale she had read,
A man confusedly in a half dream
As though some other name ran in his head.
She is foremost of those that I would hear praised.

I will talk no more of books or the long war
But walk by the dry thorn until I have found
Some beggar sheltering from the wind, and there
Manage the talk until her name come round.

If there be rags enough he will know her name
And be well pleased remembering it, for in the old days,
Though she had young men's praise and old men's blame
Among the poor both old and young gave her praise.

MEN IMPROVE WITH THE YEARS
by W. B. Yeats

I am worn out with dreams;
A weather-worn, marble triton
Among the streams;
And all day long I look
Upon this lady's beauty
As though I had found in a book
A pictured beauty,
Pleased to have filled the eyes
Or the discerning ears,
Delighted to be but wise,
For men improve with the years;
And yet, and yet,
Is this my dream, or the truth?
O would that we had met
When I had my burning youth!
But I grow old among dreams,
A weather-worn, marble triton
Among the streams.

From THE LIFE & TIMES OF JAMES CLARENCE MANGAN
by J. O'Donaghue

THE FIRST ENCOUNTER

I well remember that, on the very evening of the intro-
duction, a presentiment of over-shadowing evil hung like a
cloud above my spirit. I saw, as on the glass of a magic mirror,
the form and character of the change that was about to be
wrought upon the spirit of my dream. Those who are familiar with presentiments know that earlier or later they will
be realized. So, alas! it was with me. Shape and verification
were speedily given to the outlines of my vague imaginings.

HE INTRODUCES HER TO A FRIEND

I tried to summon a sufficient share of philosophy to assist
me in sustaining the tremendous shock thus inflicted on me.
In vain! in vain! The iron had found its way into my soul.
There it rankled and festered; the decree had gone out, and
I was thenceforth condemned to be the miserable victim of
my own confidingness and the treachery of others. Possibly
I might live – might bear about with me the burthen of my
agony for long years to come, but my peace was everlastingly
blasted, and the common atmosphere of this world, health
and life to others must be for me impregnated with invisible
poison. The denunciatory handwriting had been traced along
the wall of my destiny; the kingdom of my affections had
been taken from me and transferred to a rival. Not, indeed,
that I had been weighed in the balance and found wanting.
No! fonder, truer, madder love than mine had never
streamed in lightning through the veins of man. I had loved
with all the intense fervour attributed only to the heroes of
romance, and here was my requital! ... Would not any other
in my circumstances have stabbed the faithless fair to the
heart, or despatched a bullet through the brain of his perfid-

ious rival? I alone saw how futile such a proceeding must be. Uppermost in my mind floated a sense of loathing inexpressible ... I wrapped up my heart in the folds of bitterest scorn – this was all, and enough. No thought, no shadow of a thought of vengeance hovered within the sphere of my meditations for the future ... I was much too proud to be revengeful. Strange idiosyncrasy of mine! Yet not wholly unparalleled ... The combination of love with despair probably contributes the perfect measure of human wretchedness. ... Weeks and months wheeled onwards, but generated no alteration in me unless for the worse. I had drunk deeply of the waters of bitterness, and my every sense was still saturated with the flavour of the accursed wave. There was a down-dragging weight upon my faculties – I felt myself gradually growing into the clay. I stood upon and almost sighed for the advent of the night that should see my head pillowed upon the green and quiet mould below me. What was the earth to me? Properly no more than a sepulchral dell, whose very freshest flowers were the rank, though flaunting, offspring of rottenness and corruption. I tried to look in the miraculous face of the sun, but his glory was shrouded by a pall of sack-cloth. The burial of my hopes appeared to have been followed by an eclipse of all that was bright in the universe.

On the other hand, I cherished a morbid sympathy with whatever was terrific and funereal in the operations of nature ... Often, when the whirlwind and tempest awoke, I stood out under the starless firmamental cope and longed personally to track the career of the lightning, or to envelop myself darkly in the curtains of the thundercloud. The pitiless booming of the sea against the naked rocks in winter possessed a peculiar charm for my ulcerated imagination. ...

Questionlessly, my dreams were peopled with the most horrible and hideous and misbegotten spectra that ever rioted in the desolate chambers of a madman's brain. Frequently have I started from my bed in the hollow of the night to grapple with the phantasmagoria that flitted before me, clothed in unnameable terrors. ... The house I dwelt in was in an isolated and remote quarter of the city. Solitary, silent, and prison-like it was; nevertheless a dwelling I would not have forsaken for the most brilliant pleasure-dome under the Italian heaven. To the rear of the house extended a long and narrow court-yard, partly overgrown with grass and melancholy-looking wild flowers, but flagged at the extremity, and bounded by a colossal wall. Down the entire length of this wall, which was connected with a ruined old building, descended a metal rain-spout, and I derived a diseased gratification in listening in wet weather to the cold, bleak, heavy plash, plash, plash of the rain as it fell from this spout on the flags beneath....

> Man at most is made of clay
> Woman seems a block of granite.

THE BELL
translated by Gerard Murphy

Bell of pleasant sound ringing on a windy night: I should prefer to tryst with it to trysting with a wanton woman.

From THE BRIGHT TEMPTATION
by Austin Clarke

The moon was unclouded and it shone brightly on the bed.

Credë saw again his face, his large dark eyes, timidly shining – and her anger melted. Here, indeed, was no happy-go-lucky bed-fellow full of bad thoughts and designs, but a noble, respectful youth. The curls clustered above his pale brow, and on his bashful cheek was the shadowy flush of the foxglove. She remembered Diarmuid of the Love Spot, on whom no woman could gaze without love, as the story-tellers said. His cheek, too, must have glowed with that strange hue. Never, indeed, in all her life had she seen so handsome a young man.

'Why, I believe after all,' she exclaimed, blushing too, 'that you are really afraid of me!' But there, there, you must forgive me for my anger, for I, too, was afraid and ashamed. After all we are in a strange, a difficult position, but I know now that it is no more your fault than mine; and I trust you, for I can see that you are good. We are quite safe here, though it is a long time until the dawn, so you must tell me all about yourself.'

She could not resist touching his curls lightly with her hand.

'Come, do not be so shy,' she smiled. 'Tell me all about yourself. You know, I have not even heard your name.'

Aidan felt himself on the brink of new perils, and his tongue was tied with terror. But Credë, thinking he was only shy, settled down comfortably and happily to listen, casting admiring glances as she did so at his noble features.

So that was the Pillow Talk at Ardmore.

The next moment both of them heard a bugle sound in the night. Clearly from a distance, came the rub-a-dub of galloping horses, the shouting of men, the baying of hounds.

'My husband!' exclaimed Credë, with a cry of alarm, and she sprang up in her shift.

'Quick, quick!' she gasped. 'Where are your clothes?'

'I have none,' he wailed, blurting out the dreadful truth at last. 'I have none. I – I lost them in the river,' he added, as she stamped her bare foot impatiently on the floor.

'You little fool, why didn't you tell me before now?' she said sharply, too agitated to doubt him.

She hurried behind curtains, and he heard her rummaging, searching. She had come back again, her arms full.

'These will do,' she exclaimed, out of breath. 'They are my foster-brother's and ought to fit you. Get up quickly and dress yourself.'

'But I cannot, I have nothing on!'

'Your life is in danger and mine too. Quick, get up! You can hold a sheet around you,' she added.

With a burning face the student scrambled up, keeping a sheet around him with one hand. Modestly averting her eyes, Credë held out the bundle and he grasped it with his other hand.

The shouting, talking, of men and women in the house was louder. She hurried to a door and cautiously opened it an inch.

'You have no time to dress. The women are gone. Follow me, I must get you out. Not a sound,' she whispered over her shoulder. 'And mind you do not let the shoes fall.'

Hugging the bundle, he followed her. They were in a long narrow place, heavy with the odour of sleep, and lit by a few candles. He saw the white gleam of tumbled bedclothes and chamber-pots. Dark clothes were scattered on the benches and floor.

There were sounds of running feet, of women laughing somewhere near. A voice was calling:

'Credë! Credë!'

'Coming. I'm coming now,' she answered in a loud tone.

She pulled aside a curtain and unlatched a small door. As the curtain fell back both were in darkness again.

'Quick!' she whispered. 'Give me the sheet. I cannot see you now. Down the field by the hedge and away with you into the wood. Follow the path to the swineherd's hut and ...'

Aidan could not hear the rest of what she was saying, for she had caught his arm in the darkness so that she might push him out. But at the touch of his naked flesh, Credë bit her lip, for the Devil tempted her once more. Despite the terrible danger, the haste, she succumbed in that moment of weakness to an unchaste impulse. She had already sinned by looks, and what she had seen had caused her to offend in thought against the holy purity of Ireland. She had triumphed over that temptation, but alas! her triumph was to be undone. With greater shame and contrition must she approach her next confession, for at the very moment of parting she sinned by touch.

'You are a dear,' she whispered, grinding her teeth and squeezing Aidan's arm. At the same time, with her other thumb and second finger-nail, she gave his behind a sharp pinch as he sprang through the doorway.

ON RAGLAN ROAD
by Patrick Kavanagh

On Raglan Road on an autumn day I met her first and knew
That her dark hair would weave a snare that I might one
    day rue;
I saw the danger, yet I walked along the enchanted way,
And I said, let grief be a fallen leaf at the dawning of the
    day.

On Grafton Street in November we tripped lightly along
    the ledge
Of the deep ravine where can be seen the worth of passion's
    pledge,
The Queen of Hearts still making tarts and I not making hay –
O I loved too much and by such by such is happiness thrown
    away.

I gave her gifts of the mind I gave her the secret sign that's
    known
To the artists who have known the true gods of sound and
    stone
And word and tint. I did not stint for I gave her poems to
    say.
With her own name there and her own dark hair like clouds
    over fields of May.

On a quiet street where old ghosts meet I see her walking
    now
Away from me so hurriedly my reason must allow
That I had wooed not as I should a creature made of clay –
When the angel wooes the clay he'd lose his wings at the
    dawn of day.

from ETCHED IN MOONLIGHT
by James Stephens

But in all my movements I managed to be in a position from which I could watch those two; so close in converse, so grave in their conduct of it; so alive to all that was happening about them; and yet sunk spheres below the noise and gaiety of our companions.

Her eye looked into mine, calling to me; and at the signal I left my sentence at its middle and went towards them.

Crossing the room I had a curious perception of their eyes as they watched me advancing; and, for the first time, I observed the gulf which goes about all people and which isolates each irreparably from his fellows. A sense of unreality came upon me, and, as I looked on them, I looked on mystery; and they, staring at me, saw the unknown walking to them on legs. At a stroke we had become strangers, and all the apprehension of strangers looked through our eyes.

She arose when I came within a few paces of them.

'Let us go out,' said she.

And we went out quietly.

Again I was in the open. I breathed deeply of the chill air as though drawing on a fount of life; as though striving to draw strength and sustenance and will into my mind.

But the time had come to put an end to what I thought of evasively as 'all this'; for I was loath to submit plainly to myself what 'all this' noted. I took my will in my hand, as it were, and became the will to do, I scarcely knew what; for to one unused to the discipline and use of will there is but one approach to it, and it is through anger. The first experience of willing is brutal; and it is as though a weapon of offence, a spear or club, were in one's hand; and as I walked I began to tingle and stir with useless rage.

For they were quiet, and against my latent impetuosity they opposed that massive barrier from which I lapsed back helplessly.

Excitement I understood and loved; the quicker it mounted, the higher it surged, the higher went I. Always above it, master of it. Almost I was excitement incarnate; ready for anything that might befall, if only it were heady and masterless. But the quietude of those left me like one in a void, where no wing could find a grip and where I scarce knew how to breathe.

It was now early night.

The day was finished and all that remembered the sun had gone. The wind which had stirred faintly in tall branches had lapsed to rest. No breath moved in the world, and the clouds that had hurried before were quiet now, or were journeying in other regions of the air. Clouds there were in plenty; huge, pilings of light and shade; for a great moon, burnished and thin, and so translucent that a narrowing of the eyes might almost let one peer through it, was standing far to the left; and in the spaces between the clouds there was a sharp scarce glitter of stars.

There was more than light enough to walk by; for that great disc of the heavens poured a radiance about us that was almost as bright as day.

Now as I walked the rage that had begun to stir within ceased again, and there crept into me so dull a lassitude that had death stalked to us in the field I should not have stepped from his way.

I surrendered everything on the moment; and, for the mind must justify conduct, I justified myself in the thought that nothing was worth this trouble; and that nothing was so desirable but it could be matched elsewhere, or done without.

It is true that the mind thinks only what desire dictates; and that when desire flags thought will become ignoble. My will had flagged, for I had held it too many hours as in a vice; and I was fatigued with that most terrible of exercises.

The silence of those indomitable people weighed upon me; and the silence of the night, and the chill of that large, white moon burdened me also. Therefore, when they came to talk to me, I listened peacefully; if one may term that state of surrender peace. I listened in a cowardly quietness; replying more by a movement of the hands than by words; and when words were indispensable making brief use of them.

It was she who spoke, and her tone was gentle and anxious and official:

'We have arranged to marry,' said she.

To that I made no reply.

I took the information on the surface of my mind as one receives an arrow on a shield, and I did not permit it to enter further. There, in neutral ground, the sentence lay; and there I could look on it with the aloof curiosity of one who examines an alien thing.

'They were going to get married!' Well ... But what had it to do with me? Everyone got married sometime, and they were going to get married. This was a matter in which I had no part, for they were not going to get married to me: they were going to marry each other; it was all no business of mine.

From LETTERS OF A MATCHMAKER
by John B. Keane

Knockbrack,
Tubberdarrig West

Dear Dicky,

I am now well married and scalded thanks to you. This wife of mine must think she's a cow or something. She'll only leave the bull near her once a year. What am I to do? All my pleadings is in vain. I told the curate and I told the parish priest and they spoke to her and the answer she gave was that no one came to our Divine Mother Mary and she did fine regardless. I busted in then and said I was flesh and blood and the oul' parish priest told me conduct myself and not be making a bashte of myself and to know was there no other thing in the world except corpulation I think he called it and asked me why we weren't saying the Rosary at night and know when was I at confession last or did I know the value of Sanctifying Grace. I turned to the curate and he only shrugged his shoulders the poor fellow and I could see that if he put a spake in there would be trouble for him. I got no law from the parish priest save to conduct myself and be mindful of my wife's health and feelings and to thank God for the two fine healthy children I had and not be like a stallion that was always inclined to rear up. The curate came later on his own and he had a long talk with the wife but no use. She locked the bedroom door and I could hear her praying all night. 'Twas like a monastery from that till cockcrow. 'Tis no joke being yoked as I am. Yourself is a man I sets great store by. Maybe you'd know of some way of coming around her. I have heard of Coaxiorum but you know as well as me there is no such a thing. I'll be on the lookout for word from you. You're a man that knows the ins and outs of delicate matters.

Yours faithfully,
Thady Thade Biddy Mackessy

MAN AND WIFE
by Basil Payne

Waking sometimes at night, your sleeping thigh
Lying against my own, which previously
Proclaimed its married dominance, I ply
Questions of love's discrepancies, then deviously
Evade the issue: kiss you, or fall asleep,
Trailing, like streamers, thoughts which fail to keep
Their subtle fascination when the dawn
Edges between the curtains, cold and challenging.

A LETTER TO A VERY YOUNG LADY ON
HER MARRIAGE
by Jonathan Swift

The grand affair of your life will be to gain and preserve the
friendship and esteem of your husband. You are married to
a man of good education and learning, of an excellent understanding and an exact taste. It is true, and it is happy for you,
that these qualities in him are adorned with great modesty,
a most amiable sweetness of temper, and an unusual disposi-
tion to sobriety and virtue; but neither good nature nor
virtue will suffer him to esteem you against his judgement;
and although he is not capable of using you ill, yet you will
in time grow a thing indifferent, and perhaps contemptible,
unless you can supply the loss of youth and beauty with more
durable qualities. You have but a very few years to be young
and handsome in the eyes of the world, and as few months
to be so in the eyes of a husband who is not a fool; for I
hope you do not still dream of charms and raptures, which

marriage ever did, and ever will, put a sudden end to. Besides, yours was a match of prudence and common good liking, without any mixture of that ridiculous passion which has no being but in playbooks and romances.

You must therefore use all endeavours to attain to some degree of those accomplishments which your husband most values in other people, and for which he is most valued himself. You must improve your mind by closely pursuing such a method of study as I shall direct or approve of. You must get a collection of history and travels, which I will recommend to you, and spend some hours every day in reading them, and making extracts from them if your memory be weak. You must invite persons of knowledge and understanding to an acquaintance with you, by whose conversation you may learn to correct your taste and judgement; and when you can bring yourself to comprehend and relish the good sense of others, you will arrive in time to think rightly yourself, and to become a reasonable and agreeable companion. This must produce in your husband a true rational love and esteem for you, which old age will not diminish. He will have a regard for your judgement and opinion in matters of the greatest weight; you will be able to entertain each other without a third person to relieve by finding discourse. The endowments of your mind will even make your person more agreeable to him; and when you are alone, your time will not lie heavy upon your hands for want of some trifling amusement.

As little respect as I have for the generality of your sex, it has sometimes moved me with pity to see the lady of the house forced to withdraw immediately after dinner, and this in families where there is not much drinking; as if it were an established maxim, that women are incapable of all conversation. In a room where both sexes meet, if the men are discoursing upon any general subject, the ladies never think it their business to partake in what passes, but in a separate club entertain each other with the price and choice of lace and silk, and what dresses they liked or disapproved at the church or the playhouse. And when you are among your-selves, how naturally after the first compliments do you apply your hands to each other's lappets, and ruffles, and mantuas; as if the whole business of your lives and the public concern of the world depended upon the cut or colour of your dress. As divines say, that some people take more pains to be damned than it would cost them to be saved; so your sex employ more thought, memory, and application to be fools than would serve to make them wise and useful. When I reflect on this I cannot conceive you to be human creatures, but a certain sort of species hardly a degree above a monkey; who has more diverting tricks than any of you, is an animal less mischievous and expensive, might in time be a tolerable critic in velvet and brocade, and for aught I know, would equally become them.

I can give you no advice upon the article of expense; only I think you ought to be well informed how much your husband's revenue amounts to, and be so good a computer as to keep within it in that part of the management which falls to your share; and not to put yourself in the number of those political ladies, who think they gain a great point when they have teased their husbands to buy them a new equipage, a laced head, or a fine petticoat, without once considering what long score remained unpaid to the butcher.

I desire you will keep this letter in your cabinet, and often examine impartially your whole conduct by it; and so God bless you, and make you a fair example to your sex, and a perpetual comfort to your husband and your parent.

I am, with great truth and affection, Madam, your most faithful friend and humble servant,

Dean Swift

ONCE I WAS YELLOW-HAIRED
translated by Gerard Murphy

Once I was yellow-haired, ringleted; now my head puts forth only a short grey crop.

I would rather have locks of the raven's colour grow on my head than a short hoary crop.

Courting belongs not to me, for I wile no women; tonight my hair is hoar; I shall not be as once I was.·

From LOVE AMONG THE IRISH
by Sean O'Faolain

I am a bachelor, aged 38. I am in no hurry to get married. Next September, or the September after, I will take a holiday with an object at Lisdoonvarna, County Clare. I will inform some of the priests on holiday that I am on the lookout, and that I am a bachelor of some substance who requires a wife with a dowry of a certain minimum figure. The good priests will pass the word around. In due course a girl will be selected and the wooing will proceed on a sane plane. At Christmas my people will visit her people, and her people will investigate my background, credentials and relatives. I will meet the young lady again on some such occasion as the Rugby International in Dublin during the following Easter. In due course the nuptials will take place. If I marry at 40 on the lines I have indicated I will guarantee that at 60 my wife and myself will be fonder of one another than any couple of the same age who married in their youth for what Hollywood miscalls love, but which is in fact *lustful infatuation*.

The Female

Glittering woman is a temple built upon a sewer.

I like a maid who's not afraid
But loves so well a man
She goes with him
Both out and in
And cummes him when she can.

Those arms, now bony, thin
And useless to younger men
Once caressed with skin
The limbs of princes.

Not she with traitorous kiss her Saviour stung,
Not she denied Him with unholy tongue;
She, while apostles shrank, could dangers brave,
Last at the cross and earliest at the grave.

THE MYTH OF THE DEVOURING WOMAN is not peculiar to
the Irish race, although those early queens Deirdre, Gráinne
and Maeve merrily wrought treason, crime, havoc and
disaster in the wake of their wilful lovings. In fact their
bewitchments caused men to love them long before they

151

had set eyes on them at all. Their spirits had invaded the man's soul as might moonbeams a room at night. The taboo or bond or 'geas' or philtre they had put on the man was arbitrary, and the moment the love was kindled destruction followed hot-foot.

Woman as temple and sewer is true for all male thinking and her role as sorceress, sow, enchantress and she-devil is well and fulsomely propagated. Aristotle warned against caressing a wife too much lest she be unreasonable in her demands. Montaigne, otherwise blessed with commonsense and perspective, said that to caress a woman too well was to shit in a basket and tip it over one's head. The Talmud tells us that when the serpent entangled with Eve it spurted defilement into her which infected her children. Never mind that the infection came from him.

Woman's sensuality is therefore her triumph and her downfall. Her sensual machinery can arouse man's unconscious desire and cause him to lose himself in her more radically than she ever can in him. This is the nub of that over-amplified target called 'the battle of the sexes'. If love is the re-creation of an original happiness and that happiness is founded on the mother, then the woman is more capable of delivering it to the man than he to her. This blind power of hers, this near trick depends on instinct and is the triumph of instinct over reason and can make him hate her as much as love her and often both at one and the same time. Love or no love, the sexual act is inherently disruptive.

For a country breast-fed on chastity and gullet-fed with the religion that makes Jansenism seem sportive the transgression is twice as bad. For a woman it is ten times more so. In fact considering their background I am surprised that all Irish women are not lying down on railway tracks uttering and wailing ejaculations for the oncoming train. It would be rash to hope that women have contributed as richly and as vigorously to the theme of love. But they have contributed – wild contumely, withheld desire, craven love and a sublimated sexuality that gives rein to the most fanciful and sometimes devious images. Too often they languish like Dido under the weight of doom, loss and rejection. Nor are they bold in their descriptions; they seldom describe him, they merely describe the feeling and the event as if it were a sacrament. Desire has gone underground and reappeared as something else. There is of course Molly Bloom, but she is the creation of a man. Only she boasts and raves about her indisputable power to arouse man's desire, to come-hither him and to make jest of him in the process.

Instead of pilgrimages to Mary and Joseph, and Jude, Bridget and Ita the women of Ireland ought to be down on their knees to Mister James Joyce who not only made their sexuality more patent to the world at large but who stripped from them the shackles of their own bound souls.

Inebriations of love, shadows of love, foretastes of love, but never yet the one true love.

> Keeping a mare from breaking wind
> Keeping a loose woman from lust
> Water on the bottom of a sieve
> Trusting a mad bitch
> Salt on rushes
> A settlement after marriage
> A secret to a silly woman.

> Early Irish
> Anon

My husband must be free from cowardice, and free from avarice, and free from jealousy; for I am brave in battles and combats, and it would be a discredit to my husband if I were braver than he. I am generous and a great giver of gifts, and it would be a disgrace to my husband if he were less generous than I am. And it would not suit me at all if he were jealous, for I have never denied myself the man I took a fancy to, and I never shall whatever husband I have now or may have hereafter.

> Queen Maeve

I AM EVE
translated by Gerard Murphy

I am Eve, great Adam's wife; it is I that outraged Jesus of old; it is I that stole Heaven from my children; by rights it is I that should have gone upon the Tree.

I had a kingly house at my command; grievous the evil choice that disgraced me; grievous the chastisement of crime that has withered me: alas! my hand is not clean.

It is I that plucked the apple; it overcame the control of my greed; for that, women will not cease from folly as long as they live in the light of day.

There would be no ice in any place; there would be no glistening windy winter; there would be no hell; there would be no sorrow; there would be no fear, were it not for me.

A PRAYER
by Giolla Brighde

Get for me, O Mother Mary,
A son before I go from this world.
Do not delay to put his seed into my blood,
O Womb in which the humanity of God was formed.

From THE LAMENT FOR ART O'LEARY
by Eileen O'Connell, translated by Frank O'Connor

My love and my delight,
The day I saw you first
Beside the market-house
I had eyes for nothing else
And love for none but you.
I left my father's house
And crossed the hills with you,
And it was no bad choice.
You gave me everything:
Parlours whitened for me,
Rooms painted for me,
Ovens reddened for me,
Loaves baked for me,
Roast spitted for me,
Beds made for me;
I took my ease on flock
Until the milking time
And later if I pleased.

My mind remembers
That bright spring day,
How a hat with a band of gold became you,
Your silver-hilted sword,
Your manly right hand,
Your horse on his mettle,
The foes around you
Cowed by your air
For when you rode by
On your white-nosed mare
The English bowed
To the ground before you,
Out of no love for you,
Out of their fear,

Though sweetheart of my soul,
The English killed you.

Rider of the white palms,
How a brooch became you
In a shirt of cambric!
And your hat with laces –
When you rode there,
And their streets were bare,
'Twas no love that stayed them
But hatred and fear.

My love and my calf
Of the race of the earls of Antrim
And the Barrys of Eemokilly,
A sword that became you.
A hat with a band,
A slender foreign shoe
A suit of yarn
Woven over the water.

My love and my secret
'Tis well you were suited
In a five-ribbed stocking
Your legs top-booted,
Your cornered Caroline
Your cracking whip.
Your sprightly gelding –
Oh, many's the girl
That would stop to behold you!

My love and my sweetheart,
When I come back
The little lad Conor
And Fiach the baby
Will ask me surely
Where I left their father;

I will say with anguish
'Twas in Kilnamartyr –
They will call the father
That will never answer.

My love and my darling
That I never thought dead
Till your horse came to me
With bridle trailing,
All blood from forehead
To polished saddle
Where you should be,
Sitting or standing;
I gave one leap to the threshold,
A second to the gate,
A third upon her back.

I clapped my hands
And off at a gallop,
I did not linger
Till I found you dead
By a little furze-bush,
Without pope or bishop
Or priest or cleric
One prayer to whisper,
But an old, old woman
And her cloak about you,
And your blood in torrents,
Art O'Leary,
I did not wipe it up,
I cupped it in my hands.

My love and my delight,
Rise up now beside me,
And let me lead you home!
Until I make a feast
And I shall roast your meat,

And send for company
And call the harpers in;
And I shall make your bed
Of soft and snowy sheets,
And blankets dark and rough
To warm the beloved limbs
An autumn blast has chilled.

(*His sister speaks*)

My little love, my calf!
This is the vision
That last night brought me,
In Cork all lonely
On my bed sleeping,
That the white courtyard
And the great mansion
That we two played in
As children had fallen;
Ballingeary withered,
And your hounds were silent,
Your birds were songless,
The while they found you
On the open mountain
Without priest or cleric
But an old, old woman,
And her coat about you,
When the earth caught you,
Art O'Leary,
And your life-blood stiffened
The white shirt on you.

My love and my treasure!
What fine lovely lady
From Cork of the white sails
To the bridge of Tomey
With her dowry gathered
And cows at pasture

Would sleep alone
The night they waked you?

(*Eileen O'Connell replies*)

My darling, do not believe
One word she is saying!
It is a lie
That I slept while others
Sat up and waked you –
'Twas no sleep that took me
But the children crying:
They would not close their eyes
Without me beside them.

Oh, people, do not believe
Any lying story.
There is no woman in Ireland
That had slept beside him
And borne him three children
But would cry out
After Art O'Leary
That lies dead before me
Since yesterday morning.

Grief on you, Morris!
Heart's blood and bowel's blood!
May your eyes go blind
And your knees be broken!
You killed my darling
And no man in Ireland
Will fire the shot at you!

Grief and destruction!
Morris the traitor!
That took my man from me,
Father of three children;

There are two on the hearth
And one in the womb
I shall not bring forth.

My love and my sweetness,
Art, rise up to me,
And leap upon your mare,
And ride into Macroom
And Inchigeela beyond,
Clasping your flask of wine,
One going, one coming back,
As in your father's time.

My lasting misery
I was not by your side
The time they fired the shot
To catch it in my dress
Or in my heart, what harm,
If you but reached the hills,
Rider of the ready hands.

My love and my fortune,
'Tis an evil portion
To lay for a giant,
A shroud and a coffin;
For a big-hearted hero
That fished in the hill-streams,
And drank in bright halls
With white-breasted women.

My love and my delight,
As you went out the gate,
You turned and hurried back,
And kissed your handsome sons,
You came and kissed my hand.
And said 'Eileen, rise up
And set your business straight,

For I am leaving home,
I never may return.'
I laughed at what you said,
You had said as much before.

My husband and my friend,
Master of the bright sword,
Rouse yourself from this sleep,
Put your best things on,
Put your gauntlets on,
Take your beaver hat
Yonder hangs your whip!
Your horse is at the door,
Follow the small road east
Where every bush will bend
And every stream dry up,
And man and woman bow
If things have manners yet
That have them not I fear.

My love and my delight,
'Tis not my people's death,
'Tis not my children's death
Nor Donal Mor O'Connell,
Conal that died by drowning,
Nor the girl of six and twenty
That went across the water
To be a queen's companion,
'Tis not all these I speak of
And call on with voice broken
But noble Art O'Leary,
Art of hair so golden,
Art of wit and courage,
Art the brown mare's master,
Swept last night to nothing
Here in Carriganimma –
Perish it, name and people!

My love and my treasure,
Though I bring with me
No throng of mourners
'Tis no shame for me,
For my kinsmen are wrapped in
A sleep beyond waking
In narrow coffins
Walled up in stone.

Though but for the smallpox
And the black death
And the spotted fever,
That host of riders
With bridles shaking
Would rouse the echoes,
Coming to your waking,
Art of the white breast!

Ay, could calls but wake my kindred
In Derrynane across the mountains,
And Carhen of the yellow apples,
Many a proud and stately rider,
Many a girl with spotless kerchief
Would be here before tomorrow,
Shedding tears about your body,
Art O'Leary once so merry!

My love and my secret,
Your corn is stacked,
Your cows are milking;
On me is the grief
There's no cure for in Munster.
Till Art O'Leary rise
This grief will never yield
That's bruising all my heart,
Yet shut up fast in it,
As 'twere in a locked trunk

With the key gone astray
And rust grown on the wards.

My love and my calf!
Noble Art O'Leary,
Son of Conor, son of Cady,
Son of Lewis O'Leary,
West of the valley,
And east of Greenan
(Where berries grow thickly
And nuts crowd on branches,
And apples in heaps fall
In their own season)
What wonder to any
If Iveleary lighted
And Ballingeary,
And Gugan of the saints
For the smooth-palmed rider
The huntsman unwearied
That I would see spurring
From Grenagh without halting
When quick hounds had faltered?
Oh, rider of the bright eyes
What happened you yesterday?
I thought you in my heart
When I bought you your fine clothes
One the world could not slay.

My love and my delight,
Kin of the hardy horsemen
That would hunt all the glens
Till you had turned them home
And led them to the hall
Where tables would be spread,
Sharpness being put on knives,
Roasted beef being cut,
Bacon fit to eat,

Many a rib of mutton,
Oats in plenty hanging
To set the horses neighing –
Hairy slender horses
Flanked with sturdy horseboys,
Never charged their lodging,
Nor their horses' feeding
Had they stopped a fortnight.

'Tis known to Jesus Christ
Nor cap upon my head
Nor shift against my side
Nor shoe upon my foot
Nor gear in all my house
Nor bridle for the mare
But I will spend at law;
And I'll go oversea
And plead before the king,
And if the king be deaf
I shall come back alone
To the black-blooded thief
That slew my man on me.

Oh, rider of the white palms,
Go you to Baldwin,
And face the schemer,
The bandy-legged monster
May he rot and his children
(Wishing no harm to Maire*
Yet of no love for her,
But that my mother's body
Was a bed to her for three seasons
And to me beside her).
Take my heart's love,
Dark women of the Mill

*Her twin sister married to Baldwin of Macroom

For the sharp rhymes ye shed
On the rider of the brown mare –

But cease your weeping now,
Women of the soft, wet eyes,
Till Art O'Leary drink,
Ere he go to the dark school,
Not to learn music or song
But to prop the earth and the stone.

From ULYSSES
by James Joyce

Id like to meet a man like that God not those other ruck
besides hes young those fine young men I could see down
in Margate strand bathing place from the side of the rock
standing up in the sun naked like a God or something and
then plunging into the sea with them why arent all men like
that thered be some consolation for a woman like that lovely
little statue he bought I could look at him all day long curly
head and his shoulders his finger up for you to listen theres
real beauty and poetry for you I often felt I wanted to kiss
him all over also his lovely young cock there so simply I
wouldn't mind taking him in my mouth if nobody was looking as if it was asking you to suck it so clean and white he
looked with his boyish face I would too in $\frac{1}{2}$ a minute even
if some of it went down what its only like gruel or the dew
theres no danger besides hed be so clean compared with those
pigs of men I suppose never dream of washing it from 1 years
end to the other and the most of them only thats what gives
the women the moustaches Im sure itll be grand if I can only
get in with a handsome young poet at my age Ill throw them

the 1st thing in the morning till I see if the wishcard comes
out or Ill try pairing the lady herself and see if he comes out
Ill read and study all I can find or learn a bit off by heart
if I knew who he likes so he wont think me stupid if he thinks
all women are the same and I can teach him the other part
Ill make him feel all over him till he half faints under me
then hell write about me lover and mistress publicly too with
our 2 photographs in all the papers when he becomes famous
o but then what am I going to do about him though

   no thats no way for him has he no manners nor no refinement nor no nothing in his nature slapping us behind like
that on my bottom because I didnt call him Hugh the
ignoramus that doesnt know poetry from a cabbage thats
what you get for not keeping them in their proper place pulling off his shoes and trousers there on the chair before me
so barefaced without even asking permission and standing
out that vulgar way in the half of a shirt they wear to be
admired like a priest or a butcher or those old hypocrites in
the time of Julius Caesar of course hes right enough in his
way to pass the time as a joke sure you might as well be in
bed with what with a lion God Im sure hed have something
better to say for himself an old Lion would O well I suppose
its because they were so plump and tempting in my short
petticoat he couldnt resist they excite myself sometimes its
well for men all the amount of pleasure they get off a womans
body were so round and white for them always I wished I
was one myself for a change just to try with that thing they
have swelling upon you so hard and at the same time so soft
when you touch it my uncle John has a thing long I heard
those cornerboys saying passing the corner of Marrowbone
lane my aunt Mary has a thing hairy because it was dark and
they knew a girl was passing it didnt make me blush why
should it either its only nature and he puts his thing long into
my aunt Marys hairy etcetera and turns out to be you put
the handle in a sweepingbrush men again all over they can
pick and choose what they please a married woman or a fast
widow or a girl for their different tastes like those houses

round behind Irish street no but were to be always chained
up theyre not going to be chaining me up no damn fear once
I start I tell you for stupid husbands jealousy why cant we
all remain friends over it instead of quarrelling her husband
found it out what they did together well naturally and if he
did can he undo it hes coronado anyway whatever he does
and then he going to the other mad extreme about the wife
in Fair Tyrants of course the man never even casts a 2nd
thought on the husband or wife either its the woman he
wants and he gets her what else were we given all those desires
for Id like to know I cant help it if Im young still can I its
a wonder Im not an old shrivelled hag before my time living
with him so cold never embracing me except sometimes
when hes asleep the wrong end of me not knowing I suppose
who he has any man thatd kiss a womans bottom Id throw
my hat at him after that hed kiss anything unnatural where
we havent 1 atom of any kind of expression in us all of us
the same 2 lumps of lard before ever I do that to a man
pfooh the dirty brutes the mere thought is enough I kiss the
feet of you señorita theres some sense in that didnt he kiss
our halldoor yes he did what a madman nobody understands
his cracked ideas but me still of course a woman wants to
be embraced 20 times a day almost to make her look young
no matter by who so long as to be in love or loved by some-
body if the fellow you want isnt there sometimes by the Lord
God I was thinking would I go around by the quays there
some dark evening where nobodyd know me and pick up
a sailor off the sea thatd be hot on for it and not care a pin
whose I was only to do it off up in a gate somewhere or
one of those wildlooking gipsies in Rathfarnham had their
camp pitched near the Bloomfield laundry to try and steal
our things if they could I only sent mine there a few times
for the name model laundry sending me back over and over
some old ones old stockings that blackguardlooking fellow
with the fine eyes peeling a switch attack me in the dark and
ride me up against the wall without a word or a murderer
anybody what they do themselves the fine gentlemen in their

silk hats that KC lives up somewhere this way coming out of Hardwicke lane the night he gave us the fish supper on account of winning over the boxing match of course it was for me he gave it I knew him by his gaiters and the walk and when I turned round a minute after just to see there was a woman after coming out of it too some filthy prostitute then he goes home to his wife after that only I suppose the half of those sailors are rotten again with disease O move over your big carcass out of that for the love of Mike

From TRISTRAM SHANDY
by Laurence Sterne

My Dear Brother Toby,

What I am going to say to thee is upon the nature of women, and of love-making to them; and perhaps it is as well for thee – tho' not so well for me – that thou hast occasion for a letter of instructions upon that head, and that I am able to write it to thee.

In the first place, with regard to all which concerns religion in the affair – though I perceive from a glow in my cheek, that I blush as I begin to speak to thee upon the subject, as well knowing, notwithstanding thy unaffected secrecy, how few of its offices thou neglectest – yet I would remind thee of one (during the continuance of thy courtship) in a particular manner, which I would not have omitted; and that is, never to go forth upon the enterprize, whether it be in the morning or the afternoon, without first recommending thyself to the protection of Almighty God, that he may defend thee from the evil one.

Shave the whole top of thy crown clean once at least every

four or five days, but oftener if convenient; lest in taking off thy wig before her, thro' absence of mind, she should be able to discover how much has been cut away by Time – how much by *Trim*.

– 'Twere better to keep ideas of baldness out of her fancy.

Always carry it in thy mind, and act upon it as a sure maxim, Toby –

'*That women are timid.*' And 'tis well they are – else there would be no dealing with them.

Whatever thou hast to say, be it more or less, forget not to utter it in a low soft tone of voice. Silence, and whatever approaches it, weaves dreams of midnight secrecy into the brain: For this cause, if thou canst help it, never throw down the tongs and poker.

Avoid all kinds of pleasantry and facetiousness in thy discourse with her, and do whatever lies in thy power at the same time, to keep from her all books and writings which tend thereto: there are some devotional tracts, which if thou canst entice her to read over – it will be well: but suffer her not to look into *Rabelais*, or *Scarron*, or *Don Quixote* –

– They are all books which excite laughter; and thou knowest, dear Toby, that there is no passion so serious as lust.

Stick a pin in the bosom of thy shirt, before thou enterest her parlour.

And if thou art permitted to sit upon the same sopha with her, and she gives thee occassion to lay thy hand upon hers – beware of taking it – thou canst not lay thy hand upon hers, but she will feel the temper of thine. Leave that and as many other things as thou canst, quite undetermined; by so doing, thou wilt have her curiosity on thy side; and if she is not conquered by that, and thy ASSE continues still kicking, which there is great reason to suppose – Thou must begin, with first losing a few ounces of blood below the ears, according to the practice of the ancient Scythians, who cured the most intemperate fits of the appetite by that means.

Avicenna, after this, is for having the part annointed with the syrup of hellebore, using proper evacuations and purges

– and I believe rightly. But thou must eat little or no goat's flesh, nor red deer – nor even foal's flesh by any means; and carefully abstain – that is, as much as thou canst, from peacocks, cranes, coots, didappers, and water-hens –

As for thy drink – I need not tell thee, it must be the infusion of VERVAIN and the herb HANEA, of which Aelian relates such effects – but if thy stomach palls with it – discontinue it from time to time, taking cucumbers, melons, purslane, water-lilies, woodbine, and lettice, in the stead of them.

There is nothing further for thee, which occurs to me at present –

– Unless the breaking out of a fresh war – So wishing everything dear *Toby*, for the best,

I rest thy affectionate brother,
Walter Shandy

THE YOUNG SERVING MAN
traditional ballad

O 'tis of a damsel both fair and handsome,
This story's true, or so I've been told.
By the banks of Shannon, in a lofty mansion,
Her father gathered great stores of gold,
With many a noble he strove to mate her,
But still his counsel was all as one.
For with the folly that belongs to nature,
Her mind was set on the serving man.

As those two lovers were fondly talking,
Her father heard them, and near them drew;

And when he learned what they were discoursing
In anger home then he swiftly flew;
To build a dungeon was his intention,
To part true lovers he contrived a plan,
He swore an oath by all that's high and holy
He'd part his daughter from the serving man.

So he built a dungeon all bricks and mortar,
A flight of steps, it was under-ground,
The food he gave her was bread and water,
No other comfort for her was found.
And every day he would sorely beat her,
Till to her father she thus began
'O! father, father, won't you relent now
And let me marry the serving man?'

Young Edward found out her habitation,
It was secured by an iron door.
He vowed, in spite of all the nation,
He'd gain her freedom, or rest no more.
So at his leisure he toiled with pleasure
To gain the freedom of Mary Ann;
And when at length he gained his treasure,
She cried 'My faithful young serving man!'

Said Edward, 'Now I have freed my treasure
I will be faithful to you likewise,
And for your sake I will face your father;
To see me here it will him surprise.'
When her father brought her the bread and water,
To call his daughter he thus began.
Said Edward, 'Enter, I've freed your daughter,
Put all the fault on your serving man!'

When her father found that she was vanished,
Then like a lion he soon did roar,
Saying, 'From Ireland you shall be banished,

And with my sword I will draw your gore!'
'Agreed,' said Edward, 'I freed your daughter,
I'm proud I did it, do all you can;
But forgive your treasure, I'll die with pleasure
For the one in fault is your serving man.'

When her father found him so tender-hearted,
Then down he fell on the dungeon floor,
Saying, 'No true lovers should e'er be parted
Since love can conquer an iron door.'
So now they're one, to be parted never,
And roll in riches this couple can.
This fair young lady is blessed with pleasure,
Contented with her young serving man.

From THE BEAUX' STRATAGEM, Act III
by George Farquhar

MRS SULLEN Ha! ha! ha! my dear sister, let me embrace thee!
Now we are friends indeed; for I shall have a secret of yours
as a pledge for mine. Now you'll be good for something;
I shall have you conversable in the subjects of the sex.

DORINDA But do you think that I am so weak as to fall in
love with a fellow at first sight?

MRS SULLEN Pshaw! now you spoil all; why should not we
be as free in our friendships as the men? I warrant you,
the gentleman has got to his confidant already, has avowed
his passion, toasted your health, called you ten thousand
angels, has run over your lips, eyes, neck, shape, air, and
everything in a description that warms their mirth to a
second enjoyment.

DORINDA Your hand, sister, I ain't well.

MRS SULLEN So – she's breeding already. – Come, child, up with it – hem a little – so – now tell me, don't you like the gentleman that we saw at church just now?

DORINDA The man's well enough.

MRS SULLEN Well enough! Is he not a demigod, a Narcissus, a star, the man i' the moon?

DORINDA O sister, I'm extremely ill!

MRS SULLEN Shall I send to your mother, child, for a little of her cephalic plaister to put to the soles of your feet, or shall I send to the gentleman for something for you? Come, unlace your stays, unbosom yourself. The man is perfectly a pretty fellow, I saw him when he first came into church.

DORINDA I saw him too, sister, and with an air that shone, methought, like rays about his person.

MRS SULLEN Well said: up with it!

DORINDA No forward coquette behaviour, no airs to set him off, no studied looks nor artful posture – but nature did it all –

MRS SULLEN Better and better! – one touch more – come!

DORINDA But then his looks – did you observe his eyes?

MRS SULLEN Yes, yes I did. – His eyes, well, what of his eyes?

DORINDA Sprightly, but not wandering, they seemed to view, but never gazed on anything but me. – And then his looks so humble were, and yet so noble, that they aimed to tell me that he could with pride die at my feet, though he scorned slavery anywhere else.

MRS SULLEN The physic works purely. – How d'ye find yourself now, my dear?

DORINDA Hem! much better, my dear. – O, here comes our Mercury! [*Enter* SCRUB] Well, Scrub, what news of the gentleman?

SCRUB Madam, I have brought you a packet of news.

DORINDA Open it quickly, come.

SCRUB In the first place I inquired who the gentleman was; they told me, he was a stranger. Secondly, I asked what the gentleman was; they answered and said, that they never saw him before. Thirdly, I inquired what country-man he was; they replied, 'twas more than they knew. Fourthly, I demanded whence he came; their answer was, they could not tell. And fifthly, I asked whither he went, and they replied they knew nothing of the matter – and this is all I could learn.

MRS SULLEN But what do the people say? Can't they guess?

SCRUB Why, some think he's a spy, some guess he's a mountebank; some say one thing, some another: but, for my own part, I believe he's a Jesuit.

DORINDA A Jesuit! Why a Jesuit?

RINGLETED YOUTH OF MY LOVE
by Douglas Hyde

Ringleted youth of my love,
With thy locks bound loosely behind thee,
You passed by the road above,
But you never came in to find me;

Where were the harm for you
If you came for a little to see me,
Your kiss is a wakening dew
Were I ever so ill or so dreamy.

If I had golden store
I would make a nice little boreen,
To lead straight up to his door,
The door of the house of my storeen
Hoping to God not to miss
The sound of his footfall in it,
I have waited so long for his kiss
That for days I have slept not a minute.

I thought, O my love! you were so –
As the moon is, or sun on a fountain,
And I thought after that you were snow,
The cold snow on top of the mountain;
And I thought after that, you were more
Like God's lamp shining to find me
Or the bright star of knowledge before,
And the star of knowledge behind me.

You promised me high-heeled shoes,
And satin and silk, my storeen,
And to follow me, never to lose,
Though the ocean were round us roaring
Like a bush in a gap in a wall
I am now left lonely without thee,
And this house I grow dead of, is all
That I see around or about me.

From THE STORY OF EOCHAID'S SONS
translated by Standish H. O'Grady

When they ceased from their wandering they kindled themselves a fire; they cooked them somewhat of the game, and ate till they were satisfied. But then, by operation of their meal, they were affected with great drouth and thirst, and: 'let us send one to look for water,' said they. 'I will go,' said Fergus. Away the young fellow goes in quest of water; and he lights on a well, over which he finds an old woman standing sentry. The fashion of the hag was this: blacker than coal every joint and segment of her was, from crown to ground; comparable to a wild horse's tail the grey wiry mass of hair that pierced her scalp's upper surface; with her sickle of a greenish looking tusk that was in her head, and curled till it touched her ear, she could lop the verdant branch of an oak in full bearing [i.e. acorn-laden]; blackened and smoke-bleared eyes she had; nose awry, wide-nostrilled; a wrinkled and a freckled belly, variously unwholesome; warped crooked shins, garnished with massive ankles and a pair of capacious shovels; knotty knees she had, and livid nails. The beldame's whole description in fact was disgusting. 'That's the way it is, is it?' said the lad, and: 'that's the very way,' she answered. 'Is it guarding the well thou art?' he asked, and she said: 'it is.' 'Dost thou license me to take away some water?' 'I do,' she consented, 'yet only so that I have of thee one kiss on my cheek.' 'Not so,' said he. 'Then water shall not be conceded by me.' 'My word I give,' he went on, 'that sooner than give thee a kiss I would perish of thirst!' Then the young man departed to the place where his brethren were, and told them that he had not gotten water.

Ailill started to look for some, duly reached the same well, and denied the *cailleach* a kiss. He besought her for water, but she granted him not access to the spring.

Brian, eldest of the sons, then went on the quest, and

176

equally attained to the identical well; he solicited the old thing for water, but denied her a kiss.

Fiachra went now; the spring and the *cailleach* he found both, and petitioned for water. 'I will give it,' she said, 'and give me a kiss for it.' He bestowed on her a bare touch of a kiss, and she said: 'have thou but mere contact of Tara!' and it came true: of his seed two ruled Ireland, *Dathí* and *Ailill molt* namely, but of the others' seed: of Brian's, Ailill's, Fergus's, not one.

Niall went in search of water, and came to the very well: 'Let me have water, woman!' he cried. 'I will give it,' said she, 'and bestow on me a kiss.' He answered: 'Forby giving thee a kiss, I will even hug thee!' then he bends him to embrace her, and gives her a kiss. Which operation ended, and when he looked at her, in the whole world was not a young woman of gait more graceful, in universal semblance fairer than was she; to be likened to the last-fallen snow lying in trenches every portion of her was, from crown to sole; plump and queenly forearms, fingers long and taper, straight legs of a lovely hue she had; two sandals of the white bronze betwixt her smooth and soft white feet and the earth; about her was an ample mantle of the choicest fleece, pure crimson, and in the garment a brooch of white silver; she had lustrous teeth of pearl, great regal eyes, mouth red as the rowan-berry. 'Here, woman, is a galaxy of charms,' said the young man. 'That is true indeed.' 'And who are thou?' he pursued.

'"Royal Rule" am I,' she answered and uttered this: –

'King of Tara. I am "Royal Rule"...'

THE LOVE TALKER
by Ethna Carbery

I met the Love-Talker one eve in the glen,
He was handsomer than any of our handsome young men,
His eyes were blacker than the sloe, his voice sweeter far
Than the crooning of old Kevin's pipes beyond in Coolnagar.

I was bound for the milking with a heart fair and free –
My grief! my grief! that bitter hour drained the life from
     me;
I thought him human lover, though his lips on mine were
     cold,
And the breath of death blew keen on me within his hold.

I know not what way he came, no shadow fell behind,
But all the sighing rushes swayed beneath a faery wind,
The thrush ceased its singing, a mist crept about,
We two clung together – with the world shut out.

Beyond the ghostly mist I could hear my cattle low,
The little cow from Ballina, clean as driven snow,
The dun cow from Kerry, the roan from Inisheer,
Oh, pitiful their calling – and his whispers in my ear!

His eyes were a fire; his words were a snare;
I cried my mother's name, but no help was there;
I made the blessed Sign; then he gave a dreary moan,
A wisp of cloud went floating by, and I stood alone.

Running ever through my head, is an old-time rune –
'Who meets the Love-Talker must weave her shroud soon.'
My mother's face is furrowed with the salt tears that fall,
But the kind eyes of my father are the saddest sight of all.

I have spun the fleecy lint, and now my wheel is still,
The linen length is woven for my shroud fine and chill,
I shall stretch me on the bed where a happy maid I lay –
Pray for the soul of Mairé Og at dawning of the day!

IRISH LOVE SONG
by Katharine Tynan Hinkson

Would God I were that tender apple-blossom,
    Floating and falling from the twisted bough,
To lie and faint within your silken bosom,
    As that does now!

Or would I were a little burnished apple
    For you to pluck me, gliding by so cold,
While sun and shade your robe of lawn will dapple,
    Your hair's spun gold.

Yea, would to God I were among the roses
    That lean to kiss you as you float between!
While on the lowest branch a bud uncloses
    To touch you, Queen!

Nay, since you will not love, would I were growing
    A happy daisy in the garden path
That so your silver foot might press me going,
    Even unto death!

THE BURIAL OF HUGH ROE O'DONNELL
by Thomas McGreevey

They brought
His blackening body
Here
To rest.
Princes came
Walking
Behind it.
And all Valladolid knew
And out to Simancas all knew
Where they buried Red Hugh.

SONG
by Eleanor Alexander

He climbs his lady's tower, where sail
   Cold clouds about the moon,
And at his feet the nightingale
   Sings – Sir, too soon, too soon!

He steals across his lady's park,
   He tries her secret gate,
And overhead the saucy lark
   Sings – Sir, too late, too late!

From TERENCE
by Mrs B. M. Croker

Now she began to understand why Nita had remained at home, and why she had worn her treasured blue muslin. Was she on the brink of one of her special discoveries? The next moment she hated herself for the thought; she was becoming as suspicious as old Fouché. How horrible! Was there such a thing as mental infection? Filled with contrition, she too walked forward, and held out her hand to Mr Bertram Lovell.

Mr Bertram Lovell was an idle young man; well off and well connected, if not always well behaved. He had a sharp, thin, good-looking face, reddish-brown eyes, with a surpassing gift of eloquence, supplemented by a glib and persuasive tongue. He dressed fashionably, danced admirably, and smoked incessantly. He was also a past-master in the art of flirting, and of inferring much whilst saying little. He had flirted as far as the Second Cataract and in the Temples of Karnak. He had philandered under the pines at Simla and in the valleys of Cashmere. An Atlantic liner had been the scene of a tender friendship, a Norwegian breeze had carried his soft nothings, and the languorous air of Andalusia had heard his (broken) vows. Dowagers with daughters stared straight over his head, and sensitive Benedicks bowed to him with severe formality. All the same Lovell was popular, especially with bachelors. He was a capital shot, fairly good-natured, and no niggard. Moreover, he could both see a joke and hold his tongue. He enjoyed life thoroughly – society, shooting, travelling – but above all, sunning himself in the smiles of beauty. In the varied experience of his five-and-thirty years he had never been, figuratively speaking, so sunburnt as by the dazzling loveliness of Lady Fanshawe. The shrivelled remains of his heart he laid at her feet, and she had laughed. She smiled at his sentimental speeches, and flouted his compliments. Yet he rose early in order to walk with her in the Row; he intrigued for invitations to meet her; he cut Mrs Dashaway by her commands, and threw over pressing engagements merely to adore her from a distance in the stalls.

But he had never dared to make open love to her. No, by Jove! although she was the prettiest woman in London, always cheery, charming, fascinating, and entirely wasted on old Grev, who was undeserving of such grace and beauty, and not *her* sort at all.

THE FAERY LOVER
by Moireen Fox

It was by yonder thorn I saw the faery host;
   (O low night wind, O wind of the west!)
My love rode by, there was gold upon his brow,
   And since that hour I can neither eat nor rest.

I dare not pray lest I should forget his face
   (O black north wind blowing cold beneath the sky!)
His face and his eyes shine between me and the sun:
   If I may not be with him I would rather die.

They tell me I am cursed and I will lose my soul,
   (O red wind shrieking o'er the thorn-grown dun!)
But he is my love and I go to him to-night,
   He will ride when the thorn glistens white beneath the
       moon.

He will call my name and lift me to his breast,
   (Blow soft O wind 'neath the stars of the south!)
I care not for heaven and I fear not hell
   If I have but the kisses of his proud red mouth.

From A LITTLE KEPT
by Eileen Gormanston

But this time it was altogether different. This time she had returned home with singing in her heart. This time the incredible had happened: she herself had fallen swiftly and deeply in love. He was coming to stay the first week-end after his return from a short visit to Italy, and the interval was going to be wrapped in a golden haze.

Somewhere she had read: 'Now was beginning that crazy loss of one's self, that neglect of everything but one's dramatic thoughts about the beloved.' Yes, that was it. The crazy loss, too, of all one's safeguards – for, although even now when her heart was in thrall she loved so much more mentally than physically, she had practically made up her mind.

One by one she weighed her safeguards in scales now so heavily weighted against them, and found them wanting. Her religion? She was through with that, except externally. What had she ever got from sticking to her duty but kicks and cuffs from fate? It wasn't going to be *easy* – what with the private chapel and the week-end chaplain– (she couldn't for instance, pretend to feel faint *every* time she was supposed to be going to approach the altar); but she would manage somehow.

Her mother, who had come to live with her during those shadowed years, whose companionship and sympathy had been of such untellable help to her, and whom it would kill if she knew? She must never even guess.

Her children? They were so young they would never come within measurable distance of knowing.

Her good name? Many people retained theirs undeservedly.

Her nerves? They were pretty well frazzled as it was: she was now going to give them a run for their money.

The 'perfect fear that casteth out love'? Even that didn't

function now. Those things *didn't* happen, and, anyway, there was always the river.

One simply didn't think of the future now. The present, with its newborn happiness, was all-absorbing. *Happiness!* She had forgotten what that word meant. He held hers in the hollow of his hand. Precarious? Oh no, not in *his* hand: he did so truly love her. The *things* he had said to her! The passionate yet tender, the so understanding things! And how earnestly he had assured her that if *that* happened he would never fail her.

Her footsteps held an added lightness as she walked through the gardens, wondering if this generously flowering shrub would still be at its best, if that bed of budding flowers would be making a really good splotch of colour, when he came.

One morning, about the time he was due back from Italy, she opened the paper and read: 'Accident to Milan–Paris Express. Two British believed among casualties, names not yet known.' A terror stabbed through her. Might he be one of them? Oh, God! Might he? She rushed up to her room, threw herself on her knees beside her bed, and, with tears trickling, prayed with the directness of desperate need: 'Save him. Only save him. And if You do, I promise You – I vow – that when he comes here there won't be anything that really matters. I won't do that: I won't even do *that*.'

And that afternoon came his telegram saying he was arriving by the 7.20 train on Saturday evening.

'At last!' he whispered, seizing her in his arms as the drawing room door closed on her mother and the chaplain.

'That's long enough,' she said, trying to disengage herself when his embrace had lasted about half a minute.

'Why?' he asked, astonished. 'Don't you like it?'

'Of course I like anything that brings you nearer to me. But it was one of the things I promised.'

'*Promised?* ... Promised who?'

'God.'

'*God?*'

From SUMMER NIGHT
by Elizabeth Bowen

He slipped his hand down between the brown velvet cushion
and Emma's spine, then spread the broad of his hand against
the small of her back. Looking kindly down at her closed
eyelids he went on: 'However, it all went off all right. Oh,
and there's one thing I'd like to tell you – that chap called
me a genius.'

'How would he know?' said Emma, opening her eyes.

'We never got that clear. I was rather out of my depth.
His sister was deaf...' here Robinson paused, bent down and
passed his lips absently over Emma's forehead. 'Or did I tell
you that?'

'Yes, you told me that ... Is it true that this house is blue?'

'You'll see tomorrow.'

'There'll hardly be time, darling; I shall hardly see this
house in the daylight. I must go on to – where I'm supposed
to be.'

'At any rate, I'm glad that was all O.K. They're not on
the telephone, where you're going?'

'No, it's all right; they're not on the telephone... *You'll*
have to think of something that went wrong with my car.'

'That will all keep,' said Robinson. 'Here you are.'

'Yes, here I am.' She added: 'The night was lovely,' speaking more sadly than she knew. Yes, here she was, being settled
down to as calmly as he might have settled down to a meal.
Her naivety as a lover ... She could not have said, for instance, how much the authoritative male room – the electric
clock, the sideboard, the unlit grate, the cold of the leather
chairs, – put, at every moment when he did not touch her,
a gulf between her and him. She turned her head to the window. 'I smell flowers.'

'Yes, I've got three flowerbeds.'

'Darling, for a minute could we go out?'

She moved from his touch and picked up Queenie's tea

tray and asked if she could put it somewhere else. Holding the tray (and given countenance by it) she halted in front of the photographs. 'Oh ...' she said. 'Yes. Why?' 'I wish in a way you hadn't got any children.' 'I don't see why I shouldn't have: you have.'

'Yes, I ... But Vivie and Di are not so much *like* children –'

'If they're like you,' he said, 'those two will be having a high old time, with the cat away – '

'Oh darling, I'm not the cat.'

In the kitchen (to put the tray down) she looked round: it shone with tiling and chromium and there seemed to be switches in every place. 'What a whole lot of gadgets you have,' she said. 'Look at all those electric ...' 'Yes I like them.' 'They must cost a lot of money. My kitchen's all over black-lead and smoke and hooks. My cook would hate a kitchen like this.'

'I always forget that you have a cook.' He picked up an electric torch and they went out. Going along the side of the house, Robinson played a mouse of a light on the wall. 'Look, really blue.' But she only looked absently. 'Yes – But have I been wrong to come?' He led her off the gravel on to the lawn, till they reached the edge of a bed of stocks. Then he firmly said: 'That's for you to say, my dear girl.'

'I know it's hardly a question – I hardly know you do I?'

'We'll be getting to know each other,' said Robinson.

After a minute she let go of his hand and knelt down abruptly beside the flowers: she made movements like scooping the scent up and laving her face in it – he, meanwhile, lighted a cigarette and stood looking down. 'I'm glad you like my garden,' he said. 'You feel like getting fond of the place?'

'You say you forget that I have a cook.'

'Look, sweet, if you can't get that off your mind, you'd better get in your car and go straight home ... But you will.'

'Aunt Fran's so old, too old; it's not nice. And the Major keeps thinking about the war. And the children don't think I am good; I regret that.'

'You have got a nerve,' he said, 'but I love that. You're with me. Aren't you with me? – Come out of that flower-bed.'

They walked to the brow of the lawn; the soft feather-plumes of the pampas rose up a little over her head as she stood by him overlooking the road. She shivered. 'What are all those trees?' 'The demesne – I know they burnt down the castle years ago. The demesne's great for couples.' 'What's in there?' 'Nothing, I don't think; just the ruin, a lake ...'

'I wish – '

'Now, what?'

'I wish we had more time.'

'Yes: we don't want to stay out all night.'

So taught, she smothered the last of her little wishes for consolation. Her shyness of further words between them became extreme; she was becoming frightened of Robinson's stern, experienced delicacy on the subject of love. Her adventure became the quiet practice with him. The adventure (even, the pilgrimage) died at its root, in the childish part of her mind. When he had headed her off the cytherean terrain – the leaf-drowned castle ruin, the lake – she thought for a minute he had broken her heart, and she knew now he had broken her fairytale. He seemed content – having lit a new cigarette – to wait about in his garden for a few minutes longer: not poetry but a sort of tactile wisdom came from the firmness, lawn, under their feet. The white gate-posts, the boles of beeches above the dust-whitened wall were just seen in reflected light from the town. There was no moon, but dry, tense, translucent darkness: no dew fell.

From JOHANNA
by Mrs B. M. Croker

Johanna, pale and haggard, returned home a totally different woman to the girl who had come down the boreen but two hours previously. She walked with a drooping head, and a lagging foot, till she came to the ruins, and there stood still.

These ruins were the mere gables or shells of cottages, whose owners had fled the country the year after the great famine: they were just a cluster of grey stone walls, half overgrown with ivy and Robin-round-the-hedge. It was here, on the stump of a gate pier, that Shamus had often awaited the chance passing of his sweetheart. As she halted at this spot, with two large tears slowly coursing down her face, she started violently, for a shadow seemed to flit from wall to wall, and the object of her thoughts stood before her.

Shamus' frank and handsome young face was gaunt with privation and anxiety. His merry blue eyes looked hollow and sleepless, his very voice was husky and changed as he said, 'Shevauneen, alannah, I've been watching for ye, and it's not to bid ye good-day I'm here, but goodbye.'

'Yes,' she faltered, 'I know.'

'To be sure, bad news travels with hare's feet! Well, I give that chap his earnings, as I see ye have heard below. I went to Tracy's wake, because it was a long promise to Dan Tracy – only for that I'd have been up to see ye, but I never go back on my word, for good or bad.'

'Sure, I know that, Shamus.'

'Maggie was in it, and she looked at me very ugly. The O'Rourkes were there, and all that crew, and Thady had a drop taken. We got to argufying, but no more than that, and I was off home. I was about half a mile away, when I caught sight of some fellows lying at the back of a ditch, and I knew at wance they were up to no good! So I put on a bit of spurt, and shew! they rose like crows – six of them, no less – all a pack of divil's hounds, hunting one man, and if ye heard the tongue out of them – the bawling and the shouting – 'twould terrify ye!'

'Augh, the savages!' ejaculated Johanna.

'Ay, ye may well say so. I bested the divils at the great boundary, but Thady and Tim got over somehow, and I waited for them, and took them as they came. First Tim – I caught him on the mouth, and giv' him something to bawl for! – and next Thady. Bedad, Johanna!' and he lowered his voice, 'I'm afeared I've killed *him*!'

'Yes, they say he is on the last,' she stammered, 'and, oh, Shamus, darlin', the polis is afther ye.'

'They may be afther me, but they'll never catch me alive. I just wanted one word with you. I'm for Queenstown to-morrow and America the next day; me cousin, Pat Donovan, is in New York, doing finely, and he has often asked me to go out to him. Well, I'm going now.'

'And what about your friends here?' inquired the girl tremulously.

'I got home last night, in through the back window, and talked it out with me brother Dan, and took away me savings, for passage money. I'll come back in a couple of years, as rich as a blooded gentleman!'

'But why are ye going at all?' cried Johanna, in a voice of anguish. 'Why not stay, and face it out?'

'Yes, and if Thady dies, where am I then? I wouldn't like to see meself hanged like a poacher's dog! Anyway, I could not stand being jailed up, even for wan day. I'm going away to make a fortune for you, me darlin', and to get shot of Maggie.'

'But I don't want no fortin,' she sobbed.

'Will ye wait for me, Johanna?'

'That I will so.'

'You'll be true to me, me girl, and no matter what is said or done, nor how they work around ye, yer'll never giv' in to old Timothy?'

'Never, as long as there's the breath in me,' she answered vehemently, 'I swear by the Mother of God.'

'Swear it on the cross.'

Johanna fumbled at her neck, and drew forth a shabby rosary with its little crucifix. On this she imprinted a fervent kiss.

'And ye will write to me, alannah?' continued the young man.

'Ah, sure I can't write, Shamus!'

'Well, then, ye'll have to get Mollie at the Cross to send me a letter of your words put down on paper.'

'She will do so then, and read me what you write. Oh, Shamus, asthore, it's awful to think of you so clever and learned, and writing a terrible fine hand, and reading any sort of print; and me so ignorant and no more notion of the value of a pen than the pup, and not able to talk to ye across the says, no more than them stones, an' you so smart at everything. Ye won't forget me, will ye?'

'Will I forget the heart in me body?' he cried. 'When that stops beating, I may forget ye, but never afore, Shevauneen.'

As the pair exchanged vows in the soft Irish tongue, the sun was setting in a glow of pink and gold; beyond the stern and changeless mountains, the shadows were creeping onward, the moment of parting was stealing towards them.

'Oh, if it wasn't so far away, across the water,' moaned the girl, with uplifted hands. ''Tis only the other day, I saw a crowd of people, as if they was going to a funeral, and in the middle of them there was an old woman, held on her feet between two others, and just bowed down with grief; and they told me it was not a burying at all they were afther – but from seeing a boy away to America. His mother's heart was broke, for she knew she'd never lay an eye on him again. Oh, wirra asthew, and the same grief has come to *me*! Shamus, something misdoubts me, that we two will never see one another face to face again – that there's awful trouble before us! And this very morning I was so gay, I could hardly feel the grass under me feet, and now – ' here the words choked her, and she could not articulate.

'Now, keep up yer spirits, Johanna, me darling. Sure two

years will soon roll by,' said Shamus, 'we are young yet, with all the world before us. Keep your eye on Maggie. 'Twas she set on them O'Rourkes to half-kill me; and now she's crazy, and tearing wild to save me, and hide me; cut me head and put a plaster to it! That girl's a bad egg, and so I tell ye. And, above all, I tell ye to keep *me* in yer mind.'

'And what else would I do, Shamus? Sure ye know me by this time,' and Johanna's tears fell fast.

'And here I swear,' said Shamus, and his voice shook, 'that me heart will beat true to Shevauneen Daly, until the cold clay covers it.' As he spoke, he took the beads which were hanging loosely from Johanna's hands, and kissed the little cross with impassioned devotion. Then he held Johanna in his arms for one moment, sprang over a low stone wall, and was gone like a dream – alas! as love's young dream. To his miserable and stricken sweetheart, the whole glen seemed instantly to become dark and desolate; the sun had been superseded by a soft, melancholy twilight, the atmosphere assumed an impressive stillness – a silence which was presently broken by the rattling of some displaced stones, halfway up the hill, and the sound fell upon Johanna's heart, as the earth upon a coffin.

From OVER
by Edna O'Brien

Oh my dear I would like to be something else, anything else, an albatross. In short I wish I never knew you. Or could forget. Or be a bone – you could suck it. Or a stone in the bottom of your pocket, slipped down if you like, through one of the holes in the lining and wedged into the hem more or less forever, until you threw the coat away or gave it to one of your relations. I never saw you in a coat, only in a sort of jacket, what they call an anorak. A funny word.

The first time you came to see me you were on the point of leaving as I opened the door. Leaving already. Yes you were that intrepid. So was I. You asked me where you might put your coat, or rather that anorak thing and I couldn't think, there being no hall stand. Do you remember? The room was too big for us. I remember. Seeing you sitting an ocean away, on a print-covered chair, ill at ease, young, younger than your thirty years, and I thought how I would walk across somehow or even stride across and cradle you. It was too grand the room, the upright piano, the cut-glass chandelier. I have had notions of grandeur in the past but they are vanishing. Oh my God, everything is vanishing, except you.

A younger man. I go over our years ahead; jump ahead if you will. I will be grey before you. What a humbling thing. I will dye my tresses, all my tresses. Perhaps I should experiment now with a bottle of brown dye and a little soft brush, experiment even with my hidden hairs. I must forestall you always, always. Leave no loopholes, nothing that will disappoint or disenchant you. What nonsense, when you have already gone. I don't expect to see you again unless we bump into one another. I think I am getting disappointed in you and that is good. Excellent. You told me yourself how you lied to me. You are back from your lecturing and probably thinking of getting in touch with me, probably at this very moment. Your hand on the telephone, debating, all of you debating. Now you've taken your hand away. You've put it off. You know you can, you can put it aside like a treat, a childhood treat.

I did it. I crossed the room and what you did was to feel my hair over and over again and in different ways, touch it with the palm of your hand – your drink was in your other hand (at first you refused a drink) – felt it, strands of hair with your fingers, touched it as if it were cloth, the way a child touches its favourite surfaces such as a doll or a toy.

I keep saying child. It was like that, and you staring, staring, right through me, into me.

No knowing what I surrendered that night, what I gave up. I gave up most people, and I gave up the taste for clothes and dinners and anything that could be called frivolous. I even gave up my desire to talk, to intrude or make my presence felt. I went right back, that is true, right back to the fields, so as to speak, where I grew up. All the features of that place, the simplest things, the sensations repossessed me. Crystal clear. A gate, a hasp, a water trough, the meadows and the way one can flop down into the corner of a field, a hayfield. Dew again. And the image I had was of the wetness that babies and calves and foals have when they are just born and are about to be licked, and yet I was mother.

Undoubtedly I was the mother when I gave you that soup and peeled a potato for you and cut it in half and mashed it as if you couldn't do it yourself, and you said, 'I have a poor appetite.' You thought I should have been more imposing. Even my kitchen you liked, the untidiness and the leaves in a jug. They last a long time and I am told that they are lucky.

I should have enjoyed that night, that first unplanned meeting. As a matter of fact I did, but it has been overlaid with so much else that it is like something crushed, something smothered, something at the bottom of a cupboard that has been forgotten, its very shape destroyed, its denomination ignored, and yet it is something that will always be there, except that no one will know or care about it, and no one will want to retrieve it and in the years to come if the cupboard should be cleaned out – if, for instance, the occupants are leaving – it will indeed be found but it will be so crumpled as to be useless.

I dreamt of you before I met you. That was rash. I dream of you still, quite unedifying dreams where you are embracing me and whispering and we are interrupted the way we are constantly interrupted in life. You once told me that there were only ten minutes left for us because you had to buy a piece of perspex for a painting, make sure of getting it before the shops closed. The painting was a present to you both. I feel it was a wedding present of sorts, even though you are not married. You are proud of that last, that only, bit of independence. Yes, I believe you are afraid of her. You say it's pity that holds you. But I believe that you are afraid of her and don't know it, and I believe that you love her and don't know it.

DONAL OGE: GRIEF OF A GIRL'S HEART
by Augusta Gregory

O Donal Oge, if you go across the sea,
Bring myself with you and do not forget it;
And you will have a sweetheart for fair days and market days,
And the daughter of the King of Greece beside you at night.

It is late last night the dog was speaking of you;
The snipe was speaking of you in her deep marsh.
It is you are the lonely bird through the woods;
And that you may be without a mate until you find me.

You promised me, and you said a lie to me,
That you would be before me where the sheep are flocked;
I gave a whistle and three hundred cries to you,
And I found nothing there but a bleating lamb.

You promised me a thing that was hard for you,
A ship of gold under a silver mast;

Twelve towns with a market in all of them,
And a fine white court by the side of the sea.

You promised me a thing that is not possible,
That you would give me gloves of the skin of a fish;
That you would give me shoes of the skin of a bird;
And a suit of the dearest silk in Ireland.

O Donal Oge, it is I would be better to you
Than a high, proud, spendthrift lady:
I would milk the cow; I would bring help to you;
And if you were hard pressed, I would strike a blow for you.

O, ochone, and it's not with hunger
Or with wanting food, or drink, or sleep,
That I am growing thin, and my life is shortened;
But it is the love of a young man has withered me away.

It is early in the morning that I saw him coming,
Going along the road on the back of a horse;
He did not come to me; he made nothing of me;
And it is on my way home that I cried my fill.

When I go by myself to the Well of Loneliness,
I sit down and I go through my trouble;
When I see the world and do not see my boy,
He that has an amber shade in his hair.

It was on that Sunday I gave my love to you;
The Sunday that is last before Easter Sunday.
And myself on my knees reading the Passion;
And my two eyes giving love to you for ever.

O, aya! my mother, give myself to him;
And give him all that you have in the world;
Get out yourself to ask for alms,
And do not come back and forward looking for me.

My mother said to me not to be talking with you, to-day,
Or to-morrow, or on Sunday;
It was a bad time she took for telling me that;
It was shutting the door after the house was robbed.

My heart is as black as the blackness of the sloe,
Or as the black coal that is on the smith's forge;
Or as the sole of a shoe left in white halls;
It was you put that darkness over my life.

You have taken the east from me; you have taken the west
            from me,
You have taken what is before me and what is behind me;
You have taken the moon, you have taken the sun from me,
And my fear is great that you have taken God from me!

DEATH AND THE LADY
translated by Robin Flower

Lovely lady, rein thy will.
Let my words a warning be,
Bid thy longing heart be still.
Wed no man. Remember me.

If my counsel like thee not,
Winsome beauty bright of blee,
Thou know'st not what deeds I've wrought.
Wed no man. Remember me.

If thou know'st not they are clay:
That slim form eyes may not see,

That round breast silk hides away,
Wed no man. Remember me.

Keep my counsel lest thou slip.
If love or hate men offer thee,
Hide thy heart and hoard thy lip.
Wed no man. Remember me.

Wed no man. Remember me.
I shall come thy joy to still
Though I shall not welcome be.
Lovely lady, rein thy will.

THE SONG OF CREDE, DAUGHTER OF GUARE
translated by Kuno Meyer

These are arrows that murder sleep
At every hour in the bitter-cold night:
Pangs of love throughout the day
For the company of the man from Roiny.

Great love of a man from another land
Has come to me beyond all else:
It has taken my bloom, no colour is left,
It does not let me rest.

Sweeter than songs was his speech,
Save holy adoration of Heaven's King;
He was a glorious flame, no boastful word fell from his lips,
A slender mate for a maid's side.

When I was a child I was bashful,
I was not given to going to trysts:
Since I have come to a wayward age,
My wantonness has beguiled me.

I have every good with Guare,
The King of cold Aidne:
But my mind has fallen away from my people
To the meadow at Irluachair.

There is chanting in the meadow of glorious Aidne
Around the sides of Colman's Church:
Glorious flame, now sunk in the grave
Dinertach was his name.

From ETCHED IN MOONLIGHT
by James Stephens

She was sitting in the midst of a company and on my
approach gave me her hand to kiss. I saluted it half kneeling,
and raking her eyes with a savage stare, which she returned
with quiet constancy to which I was accustomed and which
always set me wild, so that the wish I had to beat her was
only laid by the other – and overflowing – desire I had to
kiss her.

I rose to my feet, stepped some paces back, and the conversation I had interrupted recommenced.

I was intensely aware of her and of myself; but saving
for us the place was empty for me. I could feel my chin sinking to my breast; feel my eyes strained upwards in my bent
face; feel my body projecting itself against the lips I stared
at; and I knew that she was not unaware of me.

As she spoke, her eyes strayed continually to me, carelessly, irresistibly, and swung over or under me and would not look at me. She could do that while she was talking, but while she was listening she could only half do it; for when her tongue was stilled I caught her mind or her body and held her and drew her; so that, would she or would she not, she had to look at me. And I delighted in that savage impression of myself upon her; following her nerves with the cunning of one who could see within her; and guiding her, holding her, all the time to me, to me, to me. . . . And then she looked, and I was baffled anew; for her eye was as light, as calm, as inexpressive as the bright twinkle of a raindrop that hangs and shivers on a twig.

But the game was broken by a tap on my shoulder, and, at the moment, her voice stumbled on the word she was uttering, her eyes leaped into mine and looked there, and then she was talking again and merry and gracious.

THE SHIP FROM TIRNANOGE
by Emily Hickey

We two were alone by the sea:
I, and the man I loved with me.

Our eyes were glad, and our hearts beat high,
As we sat by the sea, my love and I;

Till we looked afar, and saw a ship:
Then white, white grew his ruddy lip;

And strange, strange grew his eyes that saw
Into the heart of some deep awe.

His hand that held this hand of mine
Never a token gave nor sign;

But lay as a babe's that is just dead:
And I sat still and wondered.

Nearer and nearer the white ship drew:
Who was her captain, whence her crew?

Her crew were men and women bright,
With fair eyes full of unknown light.

From far-off Tirnanoge they came,
Where they had heard my true-love's name:

The name the birds and waves had sung,
Of one who must bide for ever young.

Strong white arms let down the boat;
Song rose up from many a throat.

Glad they were who soon had won
A lovely new companion.

They lowered the boat and they entered her;
And rowed to meet their passenger:

Rowed to the tune of a music strange,
That told of joy at the heart of change.

I heard her keel on the pebbles gride,
And she waited there till the turn o' the tide;

While they kept singing, singing clear,
A song that was passing sweet to hear:

A song that bound me in a chain
Away from any thought of pain.

They paused at last in their sweet singing,
And I saw their hands were beckoning,

In a rhythm as sweet as the stillèd songs,
That passed to the air from their silent tongues.

He rose and kissed me on the face,
And left me sitting in my place,

Quiet, quiet, life and limb,
I, who was not called like him.

Into the boat he entered grave,
And the tide turned, and she rode the wave;

And I saw him sitting at the prow,
With a rose-light about his brow.

The boat drew nigh the ship again,
With all its lovely women and men.

I saw him enter the ship and stand,
His hand held in the captain's hand.

The captain wonderful to see,
With eyes a-change in depth and blee;

A-change, a-change for ever and aye,
Blue and purple, and black, and gray:

And hair like the weed that finds a home
In the heart of a trail of white sea-foam.

I wist he was no mortal man,
But he whose name is Manannan.

They sailed away, they sailed away,
Out of the day, into the day.

A QUANDARY
translated by Patrick C. Power

Oh Hugh the son of Brian,
You flower of fairest tree,
See my situation
Since Thomas visited me.

Arouse yourself to watch,
Whether with you I'll stay;
The lord of the bound of Breg
Entices me away.

Oh Hugh, to whom I sing,
If 'tis myself you seek,
Then help, oh wand of love!
To Thomas go and speak.

Tell him in broad hints
That me, as your own wife,
You intend to keep with you
For all the days of life.

Since the clever schemer
Has met me; let me say,

That though he promised honour
He's set to have his way.

You may think, but I do not,
That this lion in search of me,
This thief among the poets,
Won't force me to agree.

If I'm seduced for love,
Don't turn, dear Hugh, on me;
Even the hungry hounds of Conn
Couldn't then make me free.

Thomas often visits me
Assuming a wizard's pose,
Concealed from those that see him
Within those magic clothes.

Often at other times,
As a hawk by me he flies,
Snatching my love among the throng –
A spectre from the skies.

As a concubine in poet's cloak
He often comes in hope
With spell of druid and charm of poet
To ask me to elope.

He comes in common human form;
He comes in fairy shape;
He comes at times a spectre;
And how can I escape?

To vanquish me he comes
Like the Clan O'Neill to battle;
He sets out with full purpose
To seduce me with his prattle.

Dressed like you, dear Hugh,
To visit he arrives;
It's hard to leave the gentle beast;
He charms me with his wiles.

If you could understand
That I need help to be true;
Oh husband that wastes my love!
My head is being turned from you.

I cannot cope with both of you:
Oh Hugh, I love you with my soul
Because we're tied in marriage;
But, Thomas, my lust you stole!

Oh Thomas, if you'll listen,
I ask you to stay away;
Oh dearest and sincere one,
Don't hurt my Hugh, I pray.

Oh Thomas, courageous spirit,
Oh Costello worth the name;
Leave me! I won't betray my man!
Chasing virgins is your game.

I'm not one of those girls
Who can be lured for fun;
You've no hope of deceiving me,
Oh brightest summer sun.

Don't believe I am a whore;
I was young when I met Hugh;
'Tis ages since I knew him first;
Me you must not woo.

You're no better for your lust;
Your type and game I know;

You thief, don't you destroy me!
You laughing robber, go!

I won't relieve your lust
In spite of your flattery;
Your rank does not impress me;
Go off across the sea!

Oh son of tawny Jordan,
Oh flower of fragrant woods,
I cannot leave my Hugh
For love or cows or goods.

Since you've not seduced me,
Go back to your native art;
Exalt the name of Ireland,
Oh Neesha, precious heart!

Oh Mannanan, son of Lug,
Oh Aengus of palace bright,
Oh Siomall of worthy skills,
Oh Finbar of the wiles of night.

Oh wisdom of Cormac Mac Airt,
Oh genius of Cool's strong son,
Oh music-play, oh skill of Guaire,
Oh anger of the Hound of Conn.

Oh famous battle-smiter,
Collector of rich plunder,
Oh pool of prosperity,
Oh man of fighting thunder.

Oh steady tree of guidance,
Oh darling, dark and brave,
Oh pouring torrent, oh gush of venom,
Oh anger of violent wave.

Oh thongs of the fires of love,
Oh voice to flatter and play,
Oh warrior of Conn's own folk.
If yours I am, dare I say?

Oh Thomas of the blood of Costello,
I've reproached you well, but still
My heart is urging me
To drink your love with a will.

I bless you with all my heart,
Oh dearest friend of me;
But do not have me stray
And arouse Hugh's jealousy.

It's sad to part from you;
But look! Hugh's over there;
Hurry away, though my need is sore,
To gaze at me, don't dare.

The trickery of women has of course not gone unheralded. A monster maid called Blathnaid also loved Cuchulain and conspired with him to return and ambush her father's house when the host is away. Cuchulain and his men hide in a wood. The maid has promised to pour milk into the stream as a sign that he can come and carry her off. When he perceives the stream becoming white from milk he storms the fort, slays her father and takes her to Ulster. Her father's bard follows to get revenge. Fiction or God decree it that he finds her on the promontory of a cliff and clasping his arms around her he flings both himself and her headlong down the precipice; punishment is never lacking and these following two cases tell in robust terms what should befall any adulterous person be it man or woman:

MASSY *versus* HEADFORT
by John Philpot Curran

[In the beginning of 1803 Limerick society was much fluttered by the elopement of Mrs Massy, once the beautiful Miss Rosslewin, wife of the Rev. Charles Massy, with the Marquis of Headfort who chose to requite thus the hospitality of her husband. The case excited widespread interest and the array of legal talent on both sides was proportionately great. Amongst the defenders we find Ponsonby and Goold, while for the prosecution were men like Curran, Hoare, and Bennet – whose simile of the Cornish wrecker, when opening the case, has often been quoted. The Marquis at this time had reached the age when Antony fell to Cleopatra's charm. His riches were great and he was equally wealthy in experiences which possibly prompted the nature of the defence;

207

its callousness so fired Curran's generous indignation that 'his speech against Lord Headfort is beyond comparison the most persuasive pleading ever uttered in a case not involving national interests or public passions'.]

Who are the parties?

The plaintiff, young, amiable, of family and education. Of the generous disinterestedness of his heart you can form an opinion even from the evidence of the defendant, that he declined an alliance, which would have added to his fortune and consideration, and which he rejected for an unportioned union with his present wife. She, too, at the time, was young, beautiful, and accomplished; and felt her affection for her husband increase, in proportion as she remembered the ardour of his love and the sincerity of his sacrifice.

Look now to the defendant! – I blush to name him! I blush to name a rank which he has tarnished – and a patent which he has worse than cancelled. High in the army – high in the State – the hereditary councillor of the king – of wealth incalculable – and to this last I advert with an indignant and contemptuous satisfaction, because, as the only instrument of his guilt and shame, it will be the means of his punishment, and the source of compensation for his guilt.

Oh! how happy had it been when he arrived at the bank of the river with the ill-fated fugitive, ere yet he had committed her to that boat, of which, like the fabled bark of Styx, the exile was eternal – how happy at that moment, so teeming with misery and with shame, if you, my lord, had met him, and could have accosted him in the character of that good genius which had abandoned him. How impressively might you have pleaded the cause of the father, of the child, of the mother, and even of the worthless defendant himself. You would have said: 'Is this the requital that you are about to make for respect and kindness, and confidence in your honour? Can you deliberately expose this young man, in the bloom of life, with all his hopes before him – can you expose

208

him, a wretched outcast from society, to the scorn of a merciless world? Can you set him adrift upon the tempestuous ocean of his own passions, at this early season, when they are most headstrong; and can you cut him out from the moorings of those domestic obligations to whose cable he might ride in safety from their turbulence? Think of, if you can conceive it, what a powerful influence arises from the sense of home, from the sacred religion of the heart in quelling the passions, in reclaiming the wanderings, in correcting the discords of the human heart; do not cruelly take from him the protection of these attachments.

But if you have no pity for the father, have mercy at least upon his innocent and helpless child; do not condemn him to an education scandalous or neglected; do not strike him into that most dreadful of all human conditions, the orphanage that springs not from the grave, that falls not from the hand of Providence, or from the stroke of death, but comes before its time, anticipated and inflicted by the remorseless cruelty of parental guilt.'

Mean however, and degraded as this woman must be, she will still (if you take her with you), have strong and heavy claims upon you. The force of such claims does certainly depend upon circumstances; before, therefore, you expose her fate to the dreadful risk of your caprice or ingratitude, in mercy to her, weigh well the confidence she can place in your future justice and honour: at that future time, much nearer than you think, by what topics can her cause be pleaded to a sated appetite, to a heart that repels her, to a just judgment in which she never could have been valued or respected? Here is not the case of an unmarried woman, with whom a pure and generous friendship may insensibly have ripened into a more serious attachment, until at last her heart became too deeply pledged to be reassumed. If so circumstanced, without any husband to betray, or child to desert, or motive to restrain, except what related solely to herself, her anxiety for your happiness made her overlook every other consideration, and commit her history to your honour; in such a case, the strongest and the highest that man's imagination can suppose, in which you at least could see nothing but the most noble and disinterested sacrifice; in which you could find nothing but what claimed from you the most kind and exalted sentiment of tenderness and devotion, and respect; and in which the most fastidious rigour would find so much more subject for sympathy than blame; let me ask you, could you even in that case, answer for your own justice and gratitude?

I do not allude to the long and pitiful catalogue of paltry adventures, in which it seems your time has been employed; the coarse and vulgar succession of casual connections, joyless, loveless, and unendeared. But do you not find upon your memory some trace of an engagement of the character I have sketched? Has not your sense of what you would owe in such a case, and to such a woman, been at least once put to the test of experiment? Has it not once, at least, happened that such a woman, with all the resolution of strong faith, flung her youth, her hope, her beauty, her talent, upon your bosom, weighed you against the world, which she found but a feather in the scale, and took you as an equivalent? How did you then acquit yourself? Did you prove yourself worthy of the sacred trust reposed in you? Did your spirit so associate with hers, as to leave her no room to regret the splendid and disinterested sacrifice she had made? Did her soul find a pillow in the tenderness of yours, and a support in its firmness? Did you preserve her high in her own consciousness, proud in your admiration and friendship, and happy in your affection? You might have so acted; and the man that was worthy of her would have perished rather than not so act, as to make her delighted with having confided so sacred a trust to his honour. Did you so act? Did she feel that, however precious to your heart, she was still more exalted and honoured in your reverence and respect? Or did she find you coarse and paltry, fluttering and unpurposed, unfeeling and ungrateful? You found her a fair and blushing flower, its beauty and its fragrance bathed in the dew of heaven. Did you so tenderly transplant it, as to preserve that beauty and fragrance unimpaired? Or did you so rudely cut it, as to interrupt its nutriment, to waste its sweetness, to blast its beauty, to bow its faded and sickly head? And did you at last fling it like 'a loathsome weed away'? Send her back to her home, to her child, to her husband, to herself.

Alas! there was not one to hold such language to this noble defendant; he did not hold it to himself. But he paraded his despicable prize in his own carriage, with his own retinue, his own servants; this veteran Paris hawked his enamoured Helen from this western quarter of the island to a seaport in the eastern, crowned with the acclamations of a senseless and grinning rabble, glorying and delighted, no doubt, in the leering and scoffing admiration of grooms and ostlers, and waiters, as he passed.

In this odious contempt of every personal feeling, of public opinion, of common humanity, did he parade this woman to the seaport, whence he transported his precious cargo to a country, where her example may be less mischievous than in her own; where I agree with my learned colleague in heartily wishing he may remain with her for ever. We are too poor, too simple, too unadvanced a country, for the example of such achievements. When the relaxation of morals is the natural growth and consequence of the great progress of art and wealth, it is accompanied by a refinement that makes it less gross than shocking; but for such palliations we are at least a century too young. I advise you, therefore, most earnestly, to rebuke this budding mischief, by letting the wholesome vigour and chastisement of a liberal verdict speak what you think of its enormity.

But he has pressed another curious topic upon you. After the plaintiff had cause to suspect his designs, and the likelihood of their being fatally successful, he did not then act precisely as he ought. Gracious God! what an argument for him to dare to advance! It is saying this to him :– 'I abused your confidence, your hospitality; I laid a base plan for the seduction of the wife of your bosom; I succeeded at last, so as to throw in upon you that most dreadful of all suspicions to a man fondly attached, proud of his wife's honour, and tremblingly alive to his own; that you were possibly a dupe to the confidence in the wife, as much as in the guest. In this so pitiable distress, which I myself had studiously and deliberately contrived for you, between hope and fear, and doubt and love, and jealousy and shame; one moment shrinking from the cruelty of your suspicion; the next, fired with indignation at the facility and credulity of your acquittal; in this labyrinth of doubt, in this frenzy of suffering, you were not collected and composed; you did not act as you might have done, if I had not worked you to madness; and upon that very madness which I have inflicted upon you, upon the very completion of my guilt, and of your misery, I will build my defence. You did not act critically right, and therefore are unworthy of compensation.'

Gentlemen, can you be dead to the remorseless atrocity of such a defence! And shall not your honest verdict mark it as it deserves.

But let me go a little further; let me ask you, for I confess I have no distinct idea – What should be the conduct of a husband so placed, and who is to act critically right? Shall he lock her up, or turn her out, or enlarge or abridge her liberty of acting as she pleases? Oh, dreadful Areopagus of the tea-table! how formidable thy inquests, how tremendous thy condemnations! In the first case, he is brutal and barbarous; an odious eastern despot. In the next; what! turn an innocent woman out of his house, without evidence or proof, but merely because he is vile and mean enough to suspect the wife of his bosom and the mother of his child! Between these extremes, what intermediate degree is he to adopt? I put this question to you – Do you at this moment, uninfluenced by any passion as you now are, but cool and collected, and uninterested as you must be, do you see clearly this proper and exact line, which the plaintiff should have pursued? I much question if you do. But if you did or could, must you not say, that he was the last man from whom you should expect the coolness to discover, or the steadiness to pursue it? And yet this is the outrageous and insolent defence that is put forward to you. My miserable client, when his brain was on fire, and every fiend of hell was let loose upon his heart, should then, it seems, have placed himself before his mirror: he should have taught the stream of agony to flow decorously down his forehead; he should have composed his features to harmony; he should have writhed with grace, and groaned in melody.

But look farther to this noble defendant and his honourable defence. The wretched woman is to be successively the victim of seduction, and of slander. She, it seems, received marked attentions. Here, I confess, I felt myself not a little at a loss. The witnesses could not describe what these marked attentions were, or are. They consisted, not, if you believe the witness, that swore to them, in any personal approach, or contact whatsoever, or in any unwarrantable topics of discourse. Of what materials, then, were they composed? Why it seems a gentleman had the insolence at table to propose to her a glass of wine; and she, oh, most abandoned lady! instead of flying like an angry parrot at his head, and besmirching and bescratching him for his insolence, tamely and basely replies, 'Port, sir, if you please.'

But, gentlemen, why do I advert to this folly, this nonsense? Not surely to vindicate from censure the most innocent and the most delightful intercourse of social kindness, or harmless and cheerful courtesy, 'where virtue is, these are most virtuous'. But I am soliciting your attention, and your feeling, to the mean and odious aggravation, to the unblushing and remorseless barbarity, of falsely aspersing the wretched woman he had undone.

One good he has done, he has disclosed to you the point in which he can feel; for how imperious must that avarice be, which could resort to so vile an expedient of frugality? Yes, I will say, that, with the common feelings of a man, he would have rather suffered his thirty thousand a year to go as compensation to the plaintiff, than have saved a shilling of it by so vile an expedient of economy. He would rather have starved with her in a gaol, he would rather have sunk with her in the ocean, than have so vilified her – than have so degraded himself. . . .

The devil, it seems, has saved the noble Marquis harmless in the past; but your verdict will tell him the term of that indemnity is expired – that his old friend and banker has no more effects in his hands – and that if he draws any more upon him, he must pay his own bills himself. You will do much good by doing so: you may not enlighten his conscience, nor touch his heart; but his frugality will understand the hint. It will adopt the prudence of age, and deter him from pursuits, in which though he may be insensible of shame, he will not be regardless of expense. You will do more – you will not only punish him in his tender point, but you will weaken him in his strong one, his money. We had heard much of this noble Lord's wealth, and much of his exploits, but not much of his accomplishments or his wit; I know not if his verses have soared even to the 'poet's corner'. I have heard it said, that an ass laden with gold could find his way through the gate of the strongest city. But, gentlemen, lighten the load upon his back, and you will completely curtail the mischievous faculty of a grave animal, whose momentum lies, not in his agility, but his weight; not in the quantity of his motion but the quantity of his matter.

There is another ground on which you are called upon to give most liberal damages, and that has been laid by the unfeeling vanity of the defendant. This business has been marked by the most elaborate publicity. It is very clear that he has been allured by the glory of the chase, and not the value of the game. The poor object of his pursuit could be of no value to him, or he would not have so wantonly, and cruelly, and unnecessarily abused her. He might easily have kept this unhappy intercourse an unsuspected secret. Even if he wished for elopement, he might easily have so contrived it, that the place of her retreat would be profoundly undiscoverable.

Yet, though even the expense, a point so tender to his delicate sensibility, of concealing could not be one-fortieth of the cost of publishing her, his vanity decided him in favour of glory and publicity. By that election, he has in fact, put forward the Irish nation, and its character so often and so variously calumniated, upon its trial before the tribunal of the empire; and your verdict will this day decide whether an Irish jury can feel with justice and spirit upon a subject that involves conjugal affection and comfort, domestic honour and repose, the certainty of issue, the weight of public opinion, the gilded and presumptuous criminality of overweening rank and station.

I doubt not but he is at this moment reclined on a silken sofa, anticipating that submissive and modest verdict, by which you will lean gently on his errors; and expecting from your patriotism, no doubt, that you think again, and again, before you condemn any great portion of the immense revenue of a great absentee, to be detained in the nation that produced it, instead of being transmitted, as it ought, to be expended in the splendour of another country. He is now probably waiting for the arrival of the report of this day, which I understand a famous note-taker has been sent hither to collect. Let not the gentleman be disturbed.

Gentlemen, let me assure you, it is more, much more, the trial of you than of the noble Marquis, of which this imported recorder is at this moment collecting materials. His noble employer is now expecting a report to the following effect:– 'Such a day came to be tried at Ennis, by a special jury, the cause of Charles Massy against the most noble Marquis of Headfort. It appeared that the plaintiff's wife was young, beautiful, and captivating; the plaintiff himself, a person fond of this beautiful creature to distraction, and both doating on their child. But the noble Marquis approached her; the plume of glory nodded on his head. Not the goddess Minerva, but the goddess Venus, had lighted up his casque with "the fire that never tires, such as many a lady gay had been dazzled with before". At the first advance she trembled; at the second, she struck to the redoubted son of Mars and pupil of Venus. The jury saw it was not his fault (it was an Irish jury); they felt compassion for the tenderness of the mother's heart, and for the warmth of the lover's passion. The jury saw on one side, a young, entertaining gallant; on the other, a beauteous creature, of charms irresistible. They recollected that Jupiter had been always successful in his amours, although Vulcan had not always escaped some awkward accidents. The jury was composed of fathers, brothers, husbands, but they had not the vulgar jealousy, that views little things of that sort with rigour; and, wishing to assimilate their country in every respect to England, now that they are united to it, they, like English gentlemen, returned to their box, with a verdict of 6d. damages, and 6d. costs.'

Let this be sent to England. I promise you, your odious secret will not be kept better than that of the wretched Mrs Massy. There is not a bawdy chronicle in London, in which the epitaph which you would have written on yourselves will not be published; and our enemies will delight in the spectacle of our precocious depravity, in seeing that we can be rotten before we are ripe. I do not suppose it; I do not, cannot, will not believe it; I will not harrow up myself with the anticipated apprehension.

There is another consideration, gentlemen, which I think most imperiously demands even a vindictive reward of exemplary damages – and that is, the breach of hospitality.

To us peculiarly does it belong to avenge the violation of its altar. The hospitality of other countries is a matter of necessity or convention – in savage nations, of the first; in polished, of the latter: but the hospitality of an Irishman is not the running account of posted and ledgered courtesies, as in other countries; it springs like all his qualities, his faults, his virtues, directly from his heart. The heart of an Irishman is by nature bold, and he confides; it is tender, and he loves; it is generous, and he gives; it is social, and he is hospitable.

This sacrilegious intruder has profaned the religion of the sacred altar so elevated in our worship, so precious to our devotion: and it is our privilege to avenge the crime. You must either pull down the altar, and abolish the worship; or you must preserve its sanctity undebased. There is no alternative between the universal exclusion of all mankind from your threshold, and the most rigorous punishment of him who is admitted and betrays.

Gentlemen, I am the more disposed to feel the strongest indignation and abhorrence at this odious conduct of the defendant, when I consider the deplorable condition to which he has reduced the plaintiff, and perhaps the still more deplorable one that the plaintiff has in prospect before him. What a progress has he to travel through, before he can attain the peace and tranquillity which he has lost? How like the wounds of the body are those of the mind! how burning the fever! how painful the suppuration! how slow, how hesitating, how relapsing the process to convalescence! Through what a variety of suffering, what new scenes and changes must my unhappy client pass, ere he can re-attain, should he ever re-attain, that health of soul of which he was despoiled by the cold and deliberate machinations of this practised and gilded seducer? ...

But I confess, I feel a ten-fold solicitude when I remember that I am addressing you as my countrymen, as Irishmen, whose characters as jurors, as gentlemen, must find either honour or degradation in the result of your decision. Small as must be the distributive share of that national estimation, that can belong to so unimportant an individual as myself, yet I do own I am tremblingly solicitous for its fate. Perhaps it appears of more value to me, because it is embarked on the same bottom with yours; perhaps the community of peril, of common safety, or common wreck gives a consequence to my share of the risk, which I would not be vain enough to give it, if it were not raised to it by that mutuality. But why stoop to think at all myself, when I know that you, gentlemen of the jury – when I know that our country itself are my clients on this day, and must abide the alternative of honour or of infamy, as you shall decide. But I will not despond, I will not dare to despond. I have every trust and hope, and confidence in you. And to that hope I will add my most fervent prayer to the God of all truth and justice, so to raise and enlighten and fortify your minds, that you may so decide, as to preserve to yourselves while you live, the most delightful of all recollections – that of acting justly; and to transmit to your children the most precious of all inheritances – the memory of your virtue.

From THE KING *versus* ROBINSON, FOR BIGAMY
by Peter Burrowes, KC

[This case may be classed amongst the documents which illustrate the social life of Ireland at the beginning of the last century, the simple facts constituting one of those astounding romances which sometimes vivify the arid pages of legal records. From the mystery of its illimitable folly one thing emerges luminous – the inexhaustible kindness of the Irish heart.

The orator places the story and the scene before his hearers as if they witnessed the reality .... Livy's beautiful story of the Roman Father is not superior to this speech, as an exquisite specimen of narrative pathos.]

On a luckless morning, in the month of July, 1810, the prisoner at the bar rapped at the door of Mr Charles Berry, an eminent attorney resident on Arran Quay, in this city. He was admitted to a conference, and a long and fatal conference. Mr Berry never had known him, never had seen him, never heard that such a man was in existence; his appearance was wretched and squalid to a degree of extremity, carrying the marks, the legible marks, of misfortune and affliction. His debilitated frame and haggard looks at once recommended him to the sympathy of Mr Berry. This sympathy was kept alive and augmented by introductory letters which this man carried with him, and by a sad and instructive tale of folly and misfortune . . . .

Mr Berry at once took him under his protection, little thinking that the hand which he grappled in friendship would one day wound him where he was most vulnerable . . . . [Mr Berry] had two daughters – the one a child, the other but a few years older, now in her sixteenth year. She, gentlemen, it is, who has become the hapless heroine of the sad story of this unfortunate family. She was in her person lovely, in her manners interesting, in female accomplishments eminently cultivated, in domestic virtues and filial duty preeminent. She had an ardent and elevated mind, a warm and affectionate heart. She was the delight of her parents at home, their pride abroad, the solace of their labours and cares, and the anticipated hope and joy of their declining years. The love of offspring, the most forcible of all our instincts, is even stronger towards the female than the male child. It is wise that it should be so, it is more wanted; it is just that it should be so, it is more requited. There is no pillow on which the head of a parent, anguished by sickness or by sorrow, can so sweetly repose, as on the bosom of an affectionate daughter . . . . Mr Berry ought, perhaps, to have guarded this treasure with more jealous suspicion; perhaps he ought not to have suffered a man, acknowledging himself to have been sunk in the vortex of fashionable dissipation, to have had opportunities of converse with this young female; but, gentlemen of the jury, it is easy to be wise after experience; it is easy to suggest expedients to prevent evil after it has occurred. Is there a man of you could suspect that a married man, with four children, paralysed and forlorn, received under your hospitable roof, covered with benefits which would have kindled gratitude in the basest nature, could be guilty of meditating the infliction of such a fatal wound upon his bene-factor?... Look at him, gentlemen, at the bar of his country! Is he an object likely to engender suspicion of such a crime? You have heard the story of his shattered fortunes – could his wealth have been attractive? What could Mr Berry have dreaded from the intercourse of such a man, even if he were unmarried? But, gentlemen, it has turned out that he had means of acquiring an ascendancy over a young female mind, which were unfortunately too prevailing; he was a man of polished manners, and, though superficial, yet attrac-tive endowments; his understanding, though not sound, was not altogether uncultivated; he had a taste for the *belle-lettres*, and was an adept in music and poetry, understood drawing, was conversant in the fashionable tales of the day, and pos-sessed of all that little artillery of accomplishment which make a man agreeable, particularly in female society. Gentle-men, it sometimes happens that the same courses which viti-ate the morals improve the manners, and that the surface appears the more polished from the corruption which it covers and conceals. In the month of December, 1810, he was ordered to Cheltenham. Mrs Berry was at the time very ill, and she was prescribed also the Cheltenham waters.

Unable to accompany them, through pressure of business, Mr Berry permitted Robinson to escort wife and daughter to the springs. With the consent of her father, the young lady accepted some trifling presents.

The party returned back to Ireland in the spring, and things remained on this footing until the fatal 18th November last. I shall trace him through the melancholy occurrences of that day. Through what artifice, through what fascination, through what suggestion, by what sophistry, by what allure-ment, he must have drugged the mind of this young female, it is impossible to say. It is a moral miracle! It is out of the ordinary course of human agency. Yet so it happened, that on the eighteenth of November, he being at the time so worn down by illness that his life was in danger, with strength scarcely sufficient to admit his being carried to the carriage in the arms of the servant, he induced this young lady to accompany him; he told her parents that he was going to the hot baths, and would leave her at Mr Vigne's to hear an eminent proficient, his (Vigne's) sister, play on the pianoforte, and begged Mr Berry would indulge her with this musical gratification, as Miss Berry was considered a first-rate performer. It is impossible for me, gentlemen, to account for his influence over this young lady's mind; it would be vanity in me to attempt to explain the cause; however, he did induce her, accompanied by her sister, a child from ten to twelve years old, to go to Mr Vigne's in Nassau Street, where the prisoner had provided a clergyman, of the name of Harris, who actually did celebrate the ceremony of marriage between them; and having prevailed on her to become his wife in point of ceremony, he was carried back to his carriage, and afterwards, in Mr Berry's servant's arms, to his own bed. I am happy, gentlemen, to say, that he did not, he could not, render his crime perfect and complete. It is really a curious riddle; it surpasses anything I ever heard or read of; and but for the melancholy and afflicting distress of her injured family, it would be a matter of novel and curious inquiry to discover how he should have sought and acquired that ascendancy over her mind. It could not be a gross and sensual passion; a glance of your eye must refute the idea. What! – a sensual passion for a being such as you behold, drooping under the ravages of disease, and unable to walk to a carriage! It could not be a mercenary attachment to the object of her father's charity; it must have been some mental fascination. By what artifices that unworthy man could influence the mind of a person ten times his superior in understanding is astonishing; the means are incredible. Whether he told her of the sufferings of his youth, the ruin of his fortunes, the desertion by his wife and her ingratitude – whether his distresses excited her compassion, or whether he deluded her into the notion of his marriage being void – is quite inexplicable; but so prevalent was his power over her mind, that she would not have disputed his authority, and probably she would have more cheerfully obeyed him, if he had commanded her to give her hand to any other man. The charitable public who will hear of this trial ought to carry in their minds this extenuation – the utter impossibility that anything sensual, or vain, or mercenary, could have actuated her mind to that strange and blind obedience. And when female criticism sits in judgment upon this hapless young lady, and is about to pronounce an austere and unfeeling judgment, I hope it will be recollected that their common and primaeval parent fell under the fascination of a reptile ....

[Robinson was sentenced to seven years' transportation]

The Intemperate

BUT LOVE WOULD NOT BE LOVE if it did not slip over into
the excessive.

From RELIQUES OF IRISH POETRY
by Miss Brooke

My dearest Nanny,

I write this with the quill of a virgin goose, on paper almost
as snowy as your breast. This is a compliment justly due to
your maidenhood and innocence. It is now so long since I
saw you, that I begin to think you have forgotten me. If your
lively image treated me as unkindly as you do yourself, I
should die of despair; but, it does not desert me, sleeping or
waking, in or out of company. My companions cannot conceive what it is that makes me so pensive, they little know
the cause, and perhaps if they did, they would only laugh

at me; for if your finger aches, there are a thousand remedies prescribed for it in an instant; but, when your heart is consumed in all the tender flames of love, not one can be found to sympathize with you. I think I have already given you many proofs of the sincerity of my passion; I don't want your pity; the beggar lives on pity – I want your hand and your heart along with it, it is this alone that can make me happy, and restore my mind to that tranquillity which it knew till these unfortunate eyes of mine first met yours. A line will revive my drooping spirits, and give my soul a holiday, which it has not enjoyed since you left this place.

I am, my dearest Nanny,
Your sincere lover

From PHELIM O'TOOLE'S COURTSHIP
by William Carleton

An Irishman, however, never despairs. If he has not apparel of his own sufficiently decent to wear on his wedding-day, he borrows from a friend. Phelim and his father remembered that there were several neighbours in the village who would oblige him with a suit for the wedding; and as to the other necessary expenses, they did what their countrymen are famous for – they trusted to chance.

'We'll work ourselves out of it some way,' said Larry.

'Sure, if all fails us, we can sell the goats for the weddin' expenses. It's one comfort that Paddy Donovan must find the dinner; an' all we have to get is the whisky, the marriage-money, an' some other thrifles.'

'They say,' observed Phelim, 'that people have more luck

whin they're marrid than whin they're single. I'll have a bout at the marriage, so I will; for worse luck I can't have, if I had half a dozen wives, than I always met wid.'

'I'll go down,' observed Larry, 'to Paddy Donovan's an' send him to the priest's to give in your names to be called to-morrow. Faith, it's well that you won't have to appear, or I dunna how you'd get over it.'

'No,' said Phelim, 'that bill won't pass. You must go to the priest yourself, an' see the curate; if you go near Father O'Hara, it ud knock a plan on the head that I've invinted. I'm in the notion that I'll make the ould woman bleed agin. I'll squeeze as much out of her as 'ill bring me to America, for I'm not overly safe here; or, if all fails, I'll marry her, an' run away wid the money. It ud bring us all acrass.'

Larry's interview with the curate was but a short one. He waited on Donovan, however, before he went, who expressed himself satisfied with the arrangement, and looked forward to the marriage as certain. As for Phelim, the idea of being called to three females at the same time was one that tickled his vanity very much. Vanity where the fair sex was concerned had been always his predominant failing. He was not finally determined on marriage with any of them; but he knew that should he even escape the three, the *éclat* resulting from so celebrated a transaction would recommend him to the sex for the remainder of his life. Impressed with this view of the matter, he sauntered about as usual; saw Foodle Flatter's daughter, and understood that her uncle had gone to the priest to have his niece and worthy Phelim called the next day. But besides this hypothesis, Phelim had another, which, after all, was the real one. He hoped that the three applications would prevent the priest from calling him at all.

The priest, who possessed much sarcastic humour, on finding the name of Phelim come in as a candidate for marriage honours with three different women, felt considerably puzzled to know what he could be at. That Phelim might hoax one or two of them was very probable; but that he should have the effrontery to make him the instrument of such an affair, he thought a little too bad.

'Now,' said he to his curate, as they talked the matter over that night, 'it is quite evident that this scapegrace reckons upon our refusing to call him with any of those females tomorrow. It is also certain that not one of the three to whom he has pledged himself is aware that he is under similar obligations to the other two.'

'How do you intend to act, sir?' enquired the curate.

'Why,' said Father O'Hara, 'certainly to call him to each; it will give the business a turn for which he is not prepared. He will stand exposed, moreover, before the congregation and that will be some punishment to him.'

'I don't know as to the punishment,' replied the curate. 'If ever a human being was free from shame, Phelim is. The fellow will consider it a joke.'

'Very possible,' observed his superior; 'but I am anxious to punish this old woman. It may prevent her from uniting herself with a fellow who would on becoming master of her money, immediately abandon her – perhaps proceed to America.'

'It will also put the females of the parish on their guard against him,' said the innocent curate, who knew not that it would raise him highly in their estimation.

'We will have a scene, at all events,' said Father O'Hara; 'for I'm resolved to expose him. No blame can be attached to those whom he has duped, excepting only the old woman, whose case will certainly excite a great deal of mirth. That matters not, however; she has earned the ridicule, and let her bear it.'

It was not until Sunday morning that the three calls occurred to Phelim in a new light. He forgot that the friends of the offended parties might visit upon his proper carcass the contumely he offered to them. This, however, did not give much anxiety, for Phelim was never more in his element than when entering upon a row.

The Sunday in question was fine, and the congregation unusually large: one would think that all the inhabitants of the parish of Teernarogarah had been assembled. Most of them certainly were.

The priest, after having gone through the usual ceremonies of the Sabbath worship, excepting those with which he concludes the mass, turned round to the congregation, and thus addressed them:–

'I would not,' said he, 'upon any other occasion of this kind think it necessary to address you at all; but this is one perfectly unique, and in some degree patriarchal, because, my friends, we are informed that it was allowed in the times of Abraham and his successors to keep more than one wife. This custom is about being revived by a modern, who wants, in a rather barefaced manner, to palm himself upon us as a patriarch. And who do you think, my friends, this Irish patriarch is? Why, no other than bouncing Phelim O'Toole!'

This was received precisely as the priest had anticipated: loud were the shouts of laughter from all parts of the congregation.

'Divil a fear o' Phelim!' they exclaimed. 'He wouldn't be himself or he'd kick up a dust some way.'

'Blessed Phelim! Jist like him! Faith, he couldn't be marrid in the common coorse!'

'Arrah, whisht till we hear the name o' the happy crathur that's to be blisthered wid Phelim! The darlin's in luck, whoever she is, an' has gained a prize in the "bouncer".'

'This patriarch,' continued the priest, 'has made his selection with great judgment and discrimination. In the first place, he has pitched upon a hoary damsel of long standing in the world – one blessed with age and experience. She is qualified to keep Phelim's house well, as soon as it shall be built; but whether she will be able to keep Phelim himself is another consideration. It is not unlikely that Phelim, in imitation of his great prototypes, may prefer living in a tent. But whether she keeps Phelim or the house, one thing is certain, that Phelim will keep her money. Phelim selected this aged woman, we presume, for her judgment; for surely she who has given such convincing proof of discretion must make a useful partner to one who, like Phelim, has that virtue yet to learn. I have no doubt, however, but in a short time he will be as discreet as his teacher.'

'Blood alive! Isn't that fine language?'

'You may say that! Begad, it's himself can discoorse! What's the Protestants to that?'

'That next upon the list is one who, though a poor man's daughter, will certainly *bring property* to Phelim. There is also an aptness in this selection which does credit to the "Patriarch". Phelim is a great dancer, an accomplishment of which we do not read that the patriarchs themselves were possessed; although we certainly do read that a light heel was of a little service to Jacob. Well, Phelim carries a light heel, and the second female of his choice on this list carries a "light hand"; it is therefore but natural to suppose that, if ever they are driven to extremities, they will make light of many things which other people would consider of weighty moment. Whether Phelim and she may long remain stationary in this country is a problem more likely to be solved at the county assizes than here. It is not improbable that his Majesty may recommend the patriarch and one of his wives to try the benefit of a voyage to New South Wales, he himself graciously vouchsafing to bear their expenses.'

'Divil a lie in that, anyhow! If ever any one crossed the wather, Phelim will. Can't his reverence be funny when he plases?'

'Many a time it was prophecized for him; an' his reverence knows best.'

'Begad, Phelim's gettin' over the coals. But sure it's all the way the father an' mother reared him.'

'Tundher-an'-turf, is he goin' to be called to a pair o' them?'

'Faix, so it seems.'

'Oh, the divil's clip! Is he mad? But let us hear it out.'

'The third damsel is by no means so well adapted for Phelim as either of the other two. What she could have seen in him is another problem much more difficult than the one I have mentioned. I would advise her to reconsider the subject, and let Phelim have the full benefit of the attention she may bestow upon it. If she finds the patriarch possessed of but one virtue, except necessity, I will admit that it is pretty certain that she will soon discover the longitude, and that has puzzled the most learned men of the world. If she marries this patriarch, I think the angels who may visit him will come in shape of policemen; and that Phelim, so long as he can find a cudgel, will give them anything but a patriarchal reception is another thing of which we may rest pretty certain.

'I now publish the banns of matrimony between Phelim O'Toole of Teernarogarah and Bridget Doran of Dernascobe. If any person knows of any impediment why these two should not be joined in wedlock, they are bound to declare it.

'This Bridget Doran, my friends, is no other than my old housekeeper; but when, where, or how Phelim could have won upon her juvenile affections is one of those mysteries which is never to be explained. I dare say the match was brought about by despair on her side, and necessity on his. She despaired of getting a husband, and he had a necessity for the money. In point of age I admit she would make a very fit wife for any patriarch.'

Language could not describe the effect which this disclosure produced upon the congregation. The fancy of every one present was tickled at the idea of a union between Phelim and the old woman. It was followed by roars of laughter, which lasted several minutes.

'Oh, thin, the curse o' the crows upon him, was he only able to butther up the ould woman! Oh, *Ghe Dhiven!* that flogs. Why, it's a wondher he didn't stale the ould slip, an' make a runaway match of it! – ha, ha, ha! *Musha,* bad scran to her, but she had young notions of her own! A purty bird she picked up in Phelim! – ha, ha, ha!'

'I also publish the banns of matrimony between Phelim

O'Toole of Teernarogarah and Sally Flattery of the same place. If any of you know of any impediment why they should not be joined in wedlock, you are bound to declare it.'

The mirth rose again loud and general. Foodle Flattery, whose character was so well known, appeared so proper a father-in-law for Phelim that his selection in this instance delighted them highly.

'Betther an' betther, Phelim! More power to you! You're fixed at last. Foodle Flattery's daughter – a known thief! Well, what harm? Phelim himself has pitch on his fingers – or had, anyhow, when he was growin' up – for many a thing stuck to them. Oh, bedad, now we know what his reverence was at when he talked about the 'sizes, bad luck to them! Betune her an' the ould woman, Phelim ud be in Paradise! Foodle Flattery's daughter! Begad, she'll "bring him property", sure enough, as his reverence says.'

'I also publish the banns of matrimony between Phelim O'Toole – whom we must in future call the "Patriarch" – of Teernarogarah, and Peggy Donovan of the same place. If any of you know of any impediment in the way of their marriage, you are bound to declare it.'

'Bravo! Phelim, *acushla*. 'Tis you that's the blessed youth. Tundher-an'-whisky, did ever anybody hear of such destate? To do three o' them! Be sure the bouncer has some schame in this. Well, one would suppose Paddy Donovan an' his daughter had more sinse nor to think of sich a runagate as bouncin' Phelim.'

'No, but the pathriark! Sure, his reverence sez that we musn't call him anything agin but the pathriark! Oh, begorra, that's the name! – ha, ha, ha!'

When the mirth of the congregation had subsided, and their comments ended, the priest concluded in the following words:–

'Now, my friends, here is such a piece of profligacy as I have never, in the whole course of my pastoral duties, witnessed. It is the act of Phelim O'Toole, be it known, who did not scruple to engage himself for marriage to three females – that is, to two girls and an old woman – and who, in addition, had the effrontery to send me his name and theirs, to be given out all on the same Sunday; thus making me an instrument in his hands to hoax those who trusted in his word. That he can marry but one of them is quite clear; but that he would not scruple to marry the three, and three more to complete the half-dozen, is a fact which no one who knows him will doubt. For my part, I know not how this business may terminate. Of a truth he has contrived to leave the claims of the three females in a state of excellent confusion. Whether it raise or lessen him in their opinion, I cannot pretend to determine. I am sorry for Donovan's daughter, for I know not what greater calamity could befall any honest family than a matrimonial union with Phelim O'Toole. I trust that this day's proceedings will operate as a caution to the females of the parish against such an unscrupulous reprobate. It is for this purpose only that I publish the names given in to me. His character was pretty well known before; it is now established; and having established it, I dismiss the subject altogether.'

Phelim's fame was now nearly at its height. Never before had such a case been known; yet the people somehow were not so much astonished as might be supposed; on the contrary, had Phelim's courtship gone off like that of another man they would have felt more surprised. We need scarcely say that the 'giving out' or 'calling' of Phelim and the three damsels was spread over the whole parish before the close of that Sunday. Every one had it – man, woman and child. It was told, repeated, and improved as it went along. New circumstances were added, fresh points made out, and other *dramatis personae* brought in – all with great felicity, and quite suitable to Phelim's character.

Strongly contrasted with the amusement of the parishioners in general was the indignation felt by the three damsels and their friends. The old housekeeper was perfectly furious; so much so, indeed, that the priest gave some dark hints at the necessity of sending for a strait waistcoat. Her fellow-servants took the liberty of breaking some strong jests upon her, in return for which she took the liberty of breaking two strong churn-staves upon them. Being a remarkably strong woman for her years, she put forth her strength to such purpose that few of them went to bed without sore bones. The priest was seriously annoyed at it, for he found that his house was a scene of battle during the remainder of the day.

Sally Flattery's uncle, in the absence of her father, indignantly espoused the cause of his niece. He and Donovan each went among their friends to excite in them a proper resentment, and to form a faction for the purpose of chastising Phelim. Their chagrin was bitter on finding that their most wrathful representations of the insult sustained by their families were received with no other spirit than one of the most extravagant mirth. In vain did they rage, and fume, and swear; they could get no one to take a serious view of it. Phelim O'Toole was the author of all, and from him it was precisely what they had expected.

Phelim himself, and the father, on hearing of the occurrence after mass, were as merry as any other two in the parish. At first the father was disposed to lose his temper; but on Phelim telling him he would hear no *gosther* on the subject, he thought proper to take it in good-humour. About this time they had not more than a week's provision in the house, and only three shillings of capital. The joke of the three calls was too good a one to pass off as an ordinary affair – they had three shillings, and although it was their last, neither of them could permit the matter to escape as a dry joke. They accordingly repaired to the little public-house of the village, where they laughed at the world, got drunk, hugged each other, despised all mankind, and staggered home, ragged and merry, poor and hearty, their arms about each other's necks, perfect models of filial duty and paternal affection.

From CASTLE RACKRENT
by Maria Edgeworth

My new lady was young, as might be supposed of a lady
that had been carried off by her own consent to Scotland,
but I could only see her at the first through her veil, which,
from bashfulness or fashion, she kept over her face – 'And
am I to walk through all this crowd of people, my dearest
love?' said she to Sir Condy, meaning us servants and ten-
ants, who had gathered at the back gate – 'My dear (said
Sir Condy) there's nothing for it but to walk, or to let me
carry you as far as the house, for you see the back road's too
narrow for a carriage, and the griet piers have tumbled down
across the front approach, so there's no driving the right way
by reason of the ruins' – 'Plato, thou reasonest well!' said she,
or words to that effect, which I could no ways understand;
and again, when her foot stumbled against a broken bit of
a car wheel, she cried out – 'Angels and ministers of grace,
defend us!' Well, thought I, to be sure if she's no Jewish like
the last, she is a mad woman for certain, which is as bad:
it would have been as well for my poor master to have taken
up with poor Judy, who is in her right mind any how.
  She was dressed like a mad woman, moreover more than
like any one I ever saw afore or since, and I could not take
my eyes off her, but still followed behind her, and her feathers
on the top of her hat were broke going in at the low back
door, and she pulled out her little bottle out of her pocket
to smell to when she found herself in the kitchen and said,
'I shall faint with the heat of this odious, odious place' – 'My
dear, it's only three steps across the kitchen, and there's a fine
air if your veil was up,' said Sir Condy, and with that threw
back her veil, so that I had then a full sight of her face; she
had not at all the colour of one going to faint, but a fine complexion of her own, as I then took it to be, though her maid
told me after it was all put on; but even complexion and all
taken in, she was no way, in point of good looks, to compare

to poor Judy; and with all she had a quality toss with her; but may be it was my over partiality to Judy, into whose place I may say she stept, that made me notice all this. – To do her justice, however, she was, when we came to know her better, very liberal in her house-keeping, nothing at all of the Skin-flint in her; she left every thing to the house-keeper, and her own maid, Mrs Jane, who went with her to Scotland, gave her the best of characters for generosity; she seldom or ever wore a thing twice the same way, Mrs Jane told us, and was always pulling her things to pieces, and giving them away, never being used in her father's house to think of expense in any thing – and she reckoned, to be sure, to go on the same way at Castle Rackrent; but when I came to enquire, I learned that her father was so mad with her for running off after his locking her up, and forbidding her to think any more of Sir Condy, that he would not give her a farthing; and it was lucky for her she had a few thousands of her own, which had been left to her by a good grand-mother, and these were very convenient to begin with. My master and my lady set out in great stile; they had the finest coach and chariot and horses and liveries, and cut the greatest dash in the county, returning their wedding visits! – and it was immediately reported that her father had undertaken to pay all my master's debts, and of course all his tradesmen gave him a new credit, and every thing went on smack smooth, and I could not but admire my lady's spirit, and was proud to see Castle Rackrent again in all its glory. – My lady had a fine taste for building and furniture, and play-houses, and she turned every thing topsy-turvy, and made the bar-rack-room into a theatre, as she called it, and she went on as if she had a mint of money at her elbow; and to be sure I thought she knew best, especially as Sir Condy said nothing to it one way or the other. All he asked, God bless him! was to live in peace and quietness, and have his bottle, or his whis-key punch at night to himself. – Now this was little enough, to be sure, for any gentleman, but my lady couldn't abide the smell of the whiskey punch. – 'My dear, (says he) you liked it well enough before we were married, and why not now?' – 'My dear, (said she) I never smelt it, or I assure you I should never have prevailed upon myself to marry you.' – 'My dear, I am sorry you did not smell it, but we can't help that now,' (returned my master, without putting himself in a passion, or going out of his way, but just fair and easy helped himself to another glass, and drank it off to her good health). All this the butler told me, who was going backwards and forwards unnoticed with the jug, and hot water, and sugar, and all he thought wanting. – Upon my master's swallowing the last glass of whiskey punch, my lady burst into tears, calling him an ungrateful, base, barbarous wretch! and went off into a fit of hysterics, as I think Mrs Jane called it, and my poor master was greatly frighted, this being the first thing of the kind he had seen; and he fell straight on his knees before her, and, like a good-hearted cratur as he was, ordered the whiskey punch out of the room, and bid 'em throw open all the windows, and cursed himself, and then my lady came to herself again, and when she saw him kneeling there, bid him get up, and not forswear himself any more, for that she was sure he did not love her, nor never had: this we learnt from Mrs Jane, who was the only person left present at all this – 'My dear, (returns my master, thinking to be sure of Judy, as well he might) whoever told you so is an incendiary, and I'll have 'em turned out of the house this minute, if you'll only let me know which of them it was.' – 'Told me what?' says my lady, starting upright in her chair. – 'Nothing, nothing at all, (said my master, seeing he had overshot himself, and that my lady spoke at random) but what you said just now that I did not love you, Bella, who told you that?' – 'My own sense,' said she, and she put her handkerchief to her face, and leant back upon Mrs Jane, and fell to sobbing as if her heart would break. – 'Why now Bella, this is very strange of you, (said my poor master) if nobody has told you nothing, what is it you are taking on for at this rate, and exposing yourself and me for this way?' – 'Oh say no more, say no more, every word you say kills me (cried

my lady, and she ran on like one, as Mrs Jane says, raving)
– Oh Sir Condy, Sir Condy! I that had hoped to find in you
"my father, brother, husband, friend".' – 'Why now faith
this is a little too much; do Bella, try to recollect yourself,
my dear; am not I your husband, and of your own chusing,
and is not that enough?' – 'Oh too much! too much!' cried
my lady, wringing her hands. – 'Why, my dear, come to
your right senses for the love of heaven – see is not the whiskey punch, jug and bowl and all, gone out of the room long
ago? what is it in the wide world you have to complain of?'
– But still my lady sobbed and sobbed, and called herself the
most wretched of women; and among other out of the way
provoking things, asked my master, was he fit company for
her, and he drinking all night. – This nettling him, which
it was hard to do, he replied, that as to drinking all night,
he was then as sober as she was herself, and that it was no
matter how much a man drank, provided it did no ways
affect or stagger him – that as to being fit company for her,
he thought himself of a family to be fit company for any
lord or lady in the land, but that he never prevented her from
seeing and keeping what company she pleased, and that he
had done his best to make Castle Rackrent pleasing to her
since her marriage, having always had the house full of visitors, and if her own relations were not amongst them, he
said, that was their own fault and their pride's fault, of which
he was sorry to find her ladyship had so unbecoming a share
– So concluding, he took his candle and walked off to his
room, and my lady was in her tantarums for three days after,
and would have been so much longer, no doubt, but some
of her friends, young ladies and cousins and second cousins,
came to Castle Rackrent, by my poor master's express in-
vitation, to see her, and she was in a hurry to get up, as Mrs
Jane called it, a play for them, and so got well, and was as
finely dressed and as happy to look at as ever, and all the
young ladies who used to be in her room dressing of her said
in Mrs Jane's hearing, that my lady was the happiest bride
ever they had seen, and that to be sure a love match was the

only thing for happiness, where the parties could any way afford it.

From THE 'ACT OF TRUTH' IN A MIDDLE-IRISH STORY
by David Greene

There was a fine, firm, righteous, generous princely king ruling over Ireland, Niall Frassach, son of Fergal. Ireland was prosperous during his reign. There was fruit and fatness, corn and milk in his time, and he had everyone settled on his own land. He called a great assembly (oenach) in Tailtiu once, and had the cream of the men of Ireland around him. Great kings and wide-eyed queens and the chiefs and nobles of the territories were ranged on the stately seats of the assembly. There were boys and jesters and the heroes of the Irish in strong eager bands racing their horses in the assembly.

While they were there, a woman came to the king carrying a boy child, and put him into the king's arms. 'For your kingship and your sovereignty', said she, 'find out for me through your ruler's truth (fir flatha) who the carnal father of this boy is, for I do not know myself. For I swear by your ruler's truth, and by the King who governs every created thing, that I have not known guilt with a man for years now.'

The king was silent then. 'Have you had playful mating with another woman?' said he, 'and do not conceal it if you have.' 'I will not conceal it,' said she; 'I have.' 'It is true (is fir),' said the king. 'That woman had mated with a man just before, and the semen which he left with her, she put it into your womb in the tumbling, so that it was begotten in your womb. That man is the father of your child, and let it be found out who he is.'

LETTER FROM OSCAR WILDE TO HIS WIFE

The Balmoral, Edinburgh
Tuesday
[postmarked 16 December 1884]

Dear and Beloved,

Here am I, and you at the Antipodes. O execrable facts, that keep our lips from kissing, though our souls are one.

What can I tell you by letter? Alas! nothing that I would tell you. The messages of the gods to each other travel not by pen and ink and indeed your bodily presence here would not make you more real: for I feel your fingers in my hair, and your cheek brushing mine. The air is full of the music of your voice, my soul and body seem no longer mine, but mingled in some exquisite ecstasy with yours. I feel incomplete without you.

Ever and ever yours
Oscar

Here I stay till Sunday.

From THE BOG OF LILIES
by Mrs M. T. Pender

God had set them apart. Others of a different complexion of mind might call it chance – circumstance – an evil hap – and set such things lightly aside for love's dear sake. But Nora, a Catholic, and an Irish Celt, endued with the intense, spiritual nature and strong religious sentiment of her race, and a supernatural faith as quick, as potent, as much a living actuality as the faith of a primitive Christian, saw behind this chance, this circumstance, this evil hap – this fiat by which their lives had been and must be forever sundered – something august, and awful and indisputable – God's will.

'For some mysterious end – it might be for the perfecting of their souls by an infinite sorrow – their lives had been sundered, and they must not attempt to fuse them against God's decree.'

This was the sum of her thinking, but not of her suffering; for it was only when she had arrived inexorably at this conclusion that she began to feel all its pain.

'I must give up my love,' she said in a low, hot, rapid voice; 'when he comes to the gate for me tonight at eleven, I must send him away – alone – back again by himself into the darkness of the night and of his life.

'When he stretches out his arms for me – when his soft, deep voice comes thrilling to me through the shadows, when he opens the gate and comes in, and takes me in his arms – I know he will do that, and he will kiss me again, whether I say yea or nay – I must tell him to go then – I must send him away – and forever.

'My God, I could not do it!' she cried suddenly, lifting her eyes heavenward, and clasping her locked hands against her breast – ' I *know* I could not! I must not meet him – I dare not! I am not one of the serene, cold women who can say "yes" or "no" to love with a quiet heart. I love him – I love him! My heart and soul – my whole being – are lost and merged in him. His will rules me, and I obey. His voice guides me, and I follow. The spell of his presence takes from me all that is distinctly mine, and I become only a part of him.

'I must not meet him. I must not see him. Oh, my dear love, I must fly from you for your own sake – for myself I care nothing.'

A minute or two longer she sat still and thought, evolving this last idea, and trying to work out of it some coherent plan of action.

She had given her vacation on the day before – country

schools usually defer their summer vacation until harvest time, in order that the pupils may be at home to help to save the grain – and so her departure from Meedianmore would excite no immediate comment. She could write to Monsignor before her month's vacation had expired, and tell him to provide another teacher – tell him – she knew not what. Her mind barely glanced at these details. There was time enough – she should have her whole life in which to arrange them while she had only a few minutes to decide its most momentous issue – to fly – to escape from – the man she loved.

There would be no train from Meedianmore station for hours yet to come. She would have to fly somewhere in the meantime – anywhere – that would take her far enough away from Ever Magennis; that would carry her beyond the possibility of meeting him. She could hide somewhere – miles away – in the dark, wild bog; and take the first train from Meedianmore station at three o'clock in the morning. Or she could walk on all night, and drive all the next day, and then take the train at some distant station where she would be totally unknown, and, as she hoped, unnoticed.

Something like this flashed vaguely through her mind; but the dominating thought was simply to get away – to get away anyhow and anywhere – only surely, certainly, and without fail, to get away.

Just then she heard the clock in the parlour striking. She counted its strokes with suspended breath. Great heaven! it was ten o'clock!

She had but one short hour now. How fast the rest had flown!

'I must bid my love farewell before I go,' she said. 'I make no pretence of being strong and wise and brave, but – I will do the best I can.' And blind with tears, her body quivering so that she scarce could hold a pen, she sat down at her desk and began to write. She had now no time to consider. She wrote the words that came to her first.

'Ever, I am going away,' she wrote. 'I dare not meet you to-night, and try to say to you in person what I am now going to say – farewell! If I did I should fail once more, as I failed to-day, and I should do you a wrong that would be irreparable.

'You stand on the heights, oh, my love! You have with you honour, and you must keep its company. *My* hand must not drag you down; thus I should ill requite your love.

'Ever, God has set us apart, and we must bear our cross; we must submit to His decree. We dare not weakly throw down the burden He has laid upon us. Rather, oh, love, let us bear it steadfastly – patiently – and as best we may, unto the end.

'Our hearts, our souls, will forever unite across the silent spaces, I with you, and you with me, though our hands shall touch – never again! I will love you always. I will watch for your greatness. I will pray for your happiness. You will forever be mine, and I yours – in spirit.

'You will live nobly, oh, my darling, for my sake; for my sake, you will do your best. I, on my part, will try to shape my life, wherever it may fall, in such a way that it may be worthy of your love. Need I say that there will be no other? For your sake – love – I will bear through all my days the lily in my hand.

'Try not to think ill of me, Ever. I cannot bear that you should think I love you *little*. Rightly or wrongly, it is the greatness of my love for you that makes me fly from you.

'There are women who would sacrifice all – themselves, the world, earth, and heaven – for love's sake. It may be that they are better or nobler or grander than I. It may be that they love more. Yet to sacrifice *all* for *your sake*, would be easy – oh, God, how easy and sweet to me! – compared to the sacrifice of giving you up.

'In that lies the pain of a thousand deaths. In that lies an eternity of sorrow.

'Believe this, my Ever, and try not to think hardly of me because I fly from you; because I leave you alone to your lonely life. To me this seems the only good – the only right – and *for your dear sake* I do it.

'I am leaving this place to-night forever. Out of your love for me, do not try to follow or find me. Pray always that on earth we may never meet again.

'Yet, since God has united our souls in love in this world, yet willed us to be apart in the flesh, I have faith that, when these bodies of clay fall from us, we may be united in some other and happier sphere.

'Until then, my love, my Ever, my earthly all – farewell. – Nora.'

From SALLY CAVANAGH
by Charles J. Kickham

He looked into the sweet face which rested all unconscious on his sister's bosom. The truth dawned upon him. He knew it all now. As if by magic, all the love of that true heart was revealed to him in an instant. And his own heart opened, and love rushed into it in such a flood, that he could scarcely restrain the impulse he felt to clasp the unconscious little maiden to his breast, as a mother might a child whom she suddenly discovers to be her own. He moved the hair back from her cheek, and was stooping down to press his lips to it, but Kate kept him back.

'Don't,' said she, 'unless – '

He understood her look, and said:

'I do, Kate.'

Kate bent a glad fond look upon little Fanny's face, and kissed her herself.

'Hold her,' said she, 'till I get some water.' And she laid little Fanny's head against the breast which she hoped would be its pillow for evermore in this world, and perhaps in the next too. All this happened in less than a minute.

From A QUEEN OF MEN: GRACE O'MALLEY
by William O'Brien

'I have lived without country or kindred and among strangers who never knew a heart-beat of my real self, among clansmen who knew me less. I have lived alone, silent, choking for air and freedom. Here, at your word, the dungeon flies open, my limbs are free and a world unbounded as yonder blue canopy opens out before me. It is a world of action, triumph and love. It is a fight for all that is holiest of earth or Heaven; for faith and race against treachery and brutal might. I have a hero for my captain and your smile to light my soul into a Paradise. Oh, Nuala, you do not know how your words have changed the world for me. You who have lived amidst the worship of gallant hearts; you who have never known what a lonely, loveless world can be.'

He stopped short, as a sigh, brief and soft as that of a south wind over a bank of violets, fell on his ear. Her eyes were turned away towards the great sea that had for years lonesomely soughed around her dreams. As his voice ceased, her face turned towards him again with a frightened surprise. There was a rich flush, like that of the inmost petals of an opening rose, on her cheek, and in the tremulous dark-blue depths of her eyes the fright of a bird disturbed in a solitary ocean.

'O Nuala!' he said as he started forward, his blood in ecstasy.

From THE EMPEROR OF ICE-CREAM
by Brian Moore

On the dance floor she took him in her arms and put her cheek against his. They began to dance. 'I know,' she whispered. 'I know what you're thinking. I know why you put that key in your pocket. You're all hot and bothered. You're like me, three years ago. I like you, Gavin. And you're going down, down, down, aren't you, Gavin?'

'You're beautiful,' he whispered. He felt sexy, but also sick.

'And rotten,' she said. 'Oh, yes, you think I'm rotten. Come on, stop pressing into me. Dance a little.'

They danced, they danced past Bobby, who stood, barely moving, pressing against Imelda, his eyes shut, his wet lips open in a smile. 'Kiss me,' said Sheila Luddin. He kissed her. The whisky whirled in his head and he missed a dance step, he stumbled and she caught him. Dizzy, coloured lights blurring in front of his eyes, he saw her face, a face which blurred into pinwheels of colour. Then it came, hot, sudden and full, and he turned quickly from her, vomit rushing from his mouth. She took his hand, led him to the table and sat him down. 'I told you,' she said. 'Better not grow up. Come on, I'll drive you home.'

'I can't. Too soon. My father.'

She laughed. 'I remember that problem. All right, we'll go for a walk. You need air. Come on.'

'No.' He loved her, it was stupid to say so, but she was stunning, she was Bobby's captive and he loved her, you see, but there was vomit on his suit, he was sure he stank to high heaven of it and there was no point in her being with him now, he'd be ashamed to touch her, he was drunk and must be sober and this lovely other rotten, lost, damned soul, the only person in the whole world who understood him, must stay here and not see him reeling in the street outside. 'I love you,' he said. 'Even though you're married. What's your phone number? May I ring you up?'

246

She bent over the table top, her red hair falling down to touch the teacups. She laughed and laughed and laughed. It was horrible. She looked up, still laughing, and said: 'Just don't grow up. Don't grow up.'

If only he could think of some crushing reply, if only he could pay her back for laughing at him, pay her back for mocking something very, very serious. But as he sat there, stiff with rage and shame, his stomach heaved. He bolted for the gents'. There, kneeling amid carbolic smells, he began his night's penance.

From THE GREEN COCKADE
by Mrs M. T. Pender

'Arise, arise,' cried Elizabeth, deeply agitated, 'I forget myself! It is little fitting that you should kneel to me – a silly girl! – it is I, rather, who should go on my knees and beg you to forgive me for the perils in which I fear I have involved you.'

'Perils,' echoed M'Cabe, impetuously, 'to serve you – to give you one moment's pleasure, to earn a smile of yours, a word of approbation – I would welcome such perils every day, if they came in squadrons!'

'You are very good,' said Elizabeth, tremulously, 'but I – poor me! – I have done nothing, indeed, to deserve such devotion.'

'Miss Lockhart, you have only to look so, to claim it as your right divine, if you will pardon my saying so.'

'*If* you will get up, Mr M'Cabe,' cried Elizabeth, laughing to hide her increasing confusion, 'I will try to forgive your extravagant speeches, which are quite enough to turn my poor head.'

'But my reward?' said M'Cabe, rising, and still holding her hand, while he looked down at her with smiling eyes – 'my promised reward for redeeming *this*?' He drew forth the Green Cockade and held it towards her.

'For saving the life of that poor, beautiful girl, at such deadly risk to yourself? – What could I give you that would be sufficient?'

He drew her nearer, gently. 'Shall I tell you?'

'We met only yesterday for the first time,' she faltered, 'and though you saved my life – and hers – we are but strangers.'

'Not now,' murmured M'Cabe – 'strangers never again.'

He bent over her; his dark impassioned face overshadowed her drooping countenance for a moment, and when the sun glanced on it again through the rhododendrons, its white beauty had taken the sudden hue of a rose's heart.

'Let me see – what did I come here for?' cried the young girl, hurriedly.

'For my happiness – at the instigation of my good genius, I feel certain.'

'Then your good genius must be a river-sprite, for I came here to get a water lily to wear in my hair at dinner.'

'Let me get it for you.'

Elizabeth silently acquiesced, and they moved along the shaded bank until they reached a still, wide pool, its marges set with lilies, into which the stream spread out.

M'Cabe gathered a few snowy cups, and long, folded, waxen buds – most exquisite.

The young girl took them with a bright smile of thanks, and fastened one great chalice-spray in the bosom of the dark blue dress she wore. The other she attempted to entwine in her hair, but failed to place it to her satisfaction.

'Let me be your mirror for this occasion,' M'Cabe begged, as he took the lilies from her hand.

'You!' – with a laugh and a blush. 'You'd put my poor flowers in upside down, I know!'

'Try me! I am sure if you only look into my heart you

will find your own fair reflection there as faithfully and brightly mirrored – '

'Hush! You are a bold flatterer, Mr M'Cabe,' interrupted Elizabeth, slightly cresting up her little bronze-crowned head. 'You have contrived to say more silly things to me within the last few minutes than all the visitors at the Reagh have found heart to do within the six months, since I came home from school.'

'Pray forgive me if I have offended you! And do not brand me with the odious character of a flatterer, unless you will remember that to you, Miss Lockhart, simple truth is the most eloquent of all flattery. When I am far away in the heart of the coming strife,' pursued the young man, after a moment's pause, and with a note of sadness in his tone, 'on the battle-field, or, it may be, in the prison or the grave – wherever my fate may fall, while wrestling in that cause to which my life is pledged, some more skilful tongue may have time to breathe into your gentle ear those words which now it would be presumption in me to – '

'Hush, hush,' again interrupted Elizabeth, in an agitated tone. 'You frighten me! Must your future course of life be indeed fraught with so many dangers?'

'I should be very sorry to alarm you, Miss Lockhart, but certainly the course mapped out for me, though most to my liking, is not a path of roses.'

'Must you leave home?'

'Immediately. I have slept my last in my father's house for many a day to come.'

'And – oh, forgive my asking – you will surely trust me?'

'Trust *you*! As I would my guardian angel!'

'Then tell me if you are going to – fight?'

'Not yet; only to organise, to enlist, to recruit the army of liberty, to administer that oath of union, which is worth a life to him who gives and him who takes.'

Elizabeth sighed deeply.

'I am so glad the terrible tocsin of war has not yet sounded! for, oh! though I inherit the blood of those stern old chieftains of the Glens, I fear no pulse of their hero-hearts has fallen to my poor share. I shall be dreadfully alarmed and horrified – oh! now I know you will despise me! – if it ever happens that you, or any of my friends must go out to fight.'

M'Cabe smiled. 'To fight,' he said, 'would not be such a hard thing – even to fight and fall – if one were sure of being so sweetly remembered.'

'I must go now,' cried Elizabeth, in sudden alarm, 'I have been loitering here a long while. What a thoughtless creature I am! I have kept you late for dinner, and Sir Joel is so punctual!'

'And your flower is not yet arranged – allow me, I may never again claim so sweet a privilege!'

She bent her head gently, and the young man deftly fastened the pure, white flower among the coils of her shining hair.

'And now I must go,' said Elizabeth, hastily, 'and ungratefully leave you to find your way to the dining room alone.'

'Good-bye,' said M'Cabe, 'and when I am far away, amid toils and dangers, you will remember – '

He broke off suddenly, his voice, his lips quivering.

'Remember what?' said Elizabeth, gently.

'That I *love you*,' he was about to say. His eyes said it plainly enough, but his lips, still quivering, formed different words in a saddened tone – 'only that I twined a lily in your hair.'

'I will remember it; but surely you make choice of your slightest service. I am still less likely to forget that you saved me from death or injury; and that, at my request, you perilled both life and liberty to save another. I should be ungrateful, indeed, and unworthy, if ever I forgot these things.'

She put her fair hand in his for a moment as she spoke.

'This looks quite like a little romance,' she said, with a laugh and a blush, with a slight tremor, too, in her low tones – 'and – you know we must meet at table as if we had not seen each other. Sir Joel is strict, and would be so angry.'

'If the sunniest spot in one's life can be called a romance, this shall, indeed, be a romance to me,' answered M'Cabe, earnestly. 'In all my leisure hours I shall haunt this pool of lilies, and even when I am far away I shall be here in spirit.'

'Then I shall come here when I want to think of you,' said the young girl, with a smile and glance of bewildering sweetness.

M'Cabe made some reply – some confused, delighted half sentence, he had no idea what, and in another moment he was alone – alone, with a great joy in his heart – a warm, tender, tumultuous glow, filling all his soul with music and the whole world with light.

From THE WEARING OF THE GREEN
by Basil King

'I beg your pardon.' The girl he addressed was, he thought, gathering water-cress, for sale or for supper. She was standing midway in the stream, with the water much above her naked ankles, her dress drawn up half-way to her knees with one hand, while the other was in the very act of being stretched out to reach something. Startled exceedingly at the sound of his apology, she dropped her dress into the water, shot up from her stooping posture, straight as the rush at her naked foot, and turned to him the loveliest face he had ever seen, for a moment. Only for a moment. Next moment she turned it round again to hide her confusion, her blush, herself.

'I really beg your pardon,' he stammered, in almost as much confusion as he had caused. But shame and shyness held her dumb still. What was he to do? He was an English tourist travelling in the wild west of Ireland at a disturbed time and in a disturbed district. He had been snipe-shooting, but had lost his native guide and gillie, who had disappeared most mysteriously. (In truth, Mick Molony, hearing 'the Peelers' were on his track, ducked under in a moment.) And here he was, with night closing in, lost in a region so trackless and desolate that this young girl was the only creature he had seen or was likely to see for hours. He looked round anxiously for the house or the smoke of the house from which this naiad had come, but there was no sign of such in sight. He must do violence to his own modesty and hers or be benighted. 'I am quite ashamed to have startled and disturbed you, but I've lost my way, and I thought, perhaps, you might be so kind as to direct me into the road to Shawnkill,' taking his hat off to her back.

'Shawnkill!' in a soft and plaintive voice which harmonised with the tender autumn twilight. 'You must – you must – ' here her voice shook with suppressed laughter. The ludicrousness of carrying on a polite conversation, standing in a stream half-way up to her knees, and with her back turned doggedly to her interlocutor, struck her suddenly and shook her with laughter, which she could all the less control because of her nervousness.

'I must – ?' after waiting in perplexed suspense for a half-minute. His matter-of-fact tone brought her to in a moment.

'If you will go along down the stream till you come to a wooden bridge and wait there for a few minutes, I'll send someone to show you the way.'

'Thank you very much. I hope you will forgive my intrusion and the trouble you are so kind as to take for me. Good-night.'

'Good-night.' She waited for a minute, then peeped round to see if he was well out of the way, and then stooping picked up the poor dead bird she had thought to save. It seemed in the twilight through the motion of the current to be alive and struggling; but it had dropped dead into the water and been carried down the stream to this spot, where it was whirled round in an eddy, which gave it in the dimness the appearance of battling for life. Then she got back to the bank, dried her feet in her pocket-handkerchief, put on her stockings and boots (now and then interrupting that operation to laugh – blushing – a sweet silvery laugh), leaped up, ran along the stream till she came to a great stone wall, which she climbed with the agility of a squirrel, though embarrassed by the dead bird in her hand. Perching for breath on the top of the wall, she saw lying in wait for her below her benighted friend. It was not in human nature to forgo another glimpse of such a face in order to spare it a blush; therefore our tourist friend had retired only far enough to be out of sight of her toilet and had waited here for her with a nervous eagerness which surprised himself. Taking off his hat and keeping it off while he spoke, to express thereby the depth at once of his contrition and of his admiration he said: 'Will you pardon me once more, but I was so confused at having startled you that I wasn't quite sure whether you said the bridge was *down* the stream or *up* the stream?' though he had just followed the stream for three miles without encountering such a bridge.

'Down,' shyly abashed again, for wasn't this climbing almost as improper as wading?

'Let me help you down,' laying his gun in the grass to hold out both his hands.

'Thank you; I think *I* can manage.' However, as he persisted in holding his hands out, and as the acceptance of his help seemed a less evil than an ungraceful scramble or a hoydenish leap down, she resigned herself to his assistance. She leaped lightly down, taking but one of his hands, which led him to notice the drenched bird in the other.

From LIGHTS & SHADOWS OF IRISH LIFE
by Mrs S. C. Hall

'Say it's your wish, just say it's your wish,' exclaimed Connor, 'and then the only sorrow I'll have will be, that instead of one year you did not say a hundred, so that I might prove my love and constancy by waiting all that time. Oh, Margaret, the hope that was frozen in my heart has burst into life again, and is destroying me entirely. I – I – ' and, overpowered by his feelings, the stout and true-hearted man rushed out of the room to conceal his emotion. He soon returned, however, and, truth to say, Margaret did not see him enter without a gush of proud and happy feeling, clouded, but not overcast, by a fear which it is difficult to overcome when you feel there is a want of stability in the person upon whom your heart reposes. He looked so handsome and so animated; his lithe boyish figure had ripened into such full and graceful proportions; his manner, so softened by disappointment, was now buoyant with joy, and the tones of his voice, despite the deep rich brogue (in which after all there is something heart-warming), were so full of fervour, so cheering – the sort of voice to hasten on the morning – to call hope from the depths of despair – to wake the echoes of an enchanted cave – to talk love in – whether in sport, or the soft, low whispers of confidence and joy. His voice, I say, was the perfection of Irish voices, and no one with a heart can have listened to the richness of a well-toned Irish voice without feeling its power; at least, such as have ear for music and heart for affection; Margaret *had* both an ear and a heart, and, in good truth, if truth must be told, she felt quite as happy as her lover, and, during the remainder of the day, did not think a great deal of the obligation he had taken on himself to abstain from fights and whiskey.

From LETTERS OF A LOVE-HUNGRY FARMER
by John B. Keane.

Tubberganban House
Tubberganban

Dear Frank,

I write to you in despair. Outside the January wind howls and whines and the windows of this lonely room are never done with rattling. In the wide, open hearth my cat and my dog are serene in their slumber, their bodies lecherously stretched towards the heat of the dying fire. It is time to go to bed but the cat and dog, mute as they are, are better company than a bed which is empty and which is not now likely to suffer from mine and the jostlings of another softer body. I feel like going out into the wind and the cold and crying out my loneliness to the night, such is my overwhelming need for female company. It is not a sexual need alone. There is far more to it than that. There is a desire to share the mind and the heart as well as the body, a craving to communicate at a spiritual as well as a physical level. Since my mother died this place is lonelier than the grave during the long, callous nights of winter. There is nothing for it but the pub, the singing lounge, the dance-hall and the bingo. Even the television palls when there is no one near to share it with.

I have the odd feeling Frank, as I write this, that I am the last of my kind, that this district shall not hear such mournful sighs of sexual hunger again, that the world is catching up with me and my equals. No longer will single men inhabit these bleak, desolate, hilly places where snipe and curlew are more plentiful than people, where there is no diversion for the crusty bachelor like myself, where a man is a lost soul who has not a wife or family.

Oh how I envy you, your wife, your children and your grandchildren. What is there for me at fifty-two years of age? Is there in some remote corner of the earth the ideal companion who languishes as I do, ever-hopeful, ever-constant to the romantic ideal. I fear not. My experiences away from home lately have taught me that the seasoned, unattached females of today are the most dreadful predators since the dawn of time. They burn up vodka and gin as if they had jet engines. You wouldn't mind it if they softened them out but the opposite is the case. They become more hardened and crafty with every dollop. Many of them will drink your gin and your vodka all night and then disappear with some other fellow without a razoo to his name who has only to lift a finger. I have been led on countless times by these gold-diggers and often when I felt I was on the point of conquest I was always foiled by some sharp, sly, handsome, semi-illiterate son of a gombeenman. Whatever the formula is I don't seem to have it and yet it is possessed by seemingly retarded, ignorant hulks who have extraordinary powers over the opposite sex. There is, of course, no accounting for the tastes of women. No matter how intelligent they are a man should prepare himself for a pattern of behaviour that is mule-like in its unpredictability.

I think I'll advertise for a housekeeper. For better or for worse she'll be another human soul and this might in some small way help to alleviate my long martyrdom. The bother is that it will be next to impossible to persuade a woman to live in. This house is miles from the nearest town and the nearest neighbours are nearly half a mile away.

You wouldn't by any chance know any cute oul' doxie up there who would cater for a single gentleman. Ask Flora to be on the look-out. Meanwhile I'll advertise in the papers here.

All jokes aside I need someone around the house to keep the place tidy and to provide a decent meal now and then. From a purely financial point of view I'm fairly sound and could offer a good wage. The farm takes up most of my free time and I find if I don't go out by night that I succumb to long bouts of depression. I don't want her too young or too old. Somewhere in between would suit nicely. Surely there's a fair cut of a woman somewhere who wouldn't turn her back on a good home, a childless widow or some unfortunate creature who has been deserted by her husband. That sort of business is rampant these days. If I had a woman I wouldn't run away from her. I'd fetter her in case she might run away from me.

Sorry for these mournful outpourings. I'm sure you have enough troubles of your own. Try to spare a thought for an old friend.

Sincerely,
[John Bosco]

From JOHNNY I HARDLY KNEW YOU
by Edna O'Brien

I liken love to a great house, a mansion that once you go in, the big door shuts behind you and you have no idea, no premonition where it will all lead to. Chambers, vaults, confounded mazes, ladders, scaffolding, into darkness, out of darkness – anything.

ACKNOWLEDGEMENTS

Copyright material in this book has been included by kind permission of the following writers, publishers and literary representatives:

John Calder (Publishers) Ltd, London, for an extract from *Molloy* and a poem taken from *Collected Poems in English and French* by Samuel Beckett, both pieces translated by the author from his own original French.

Dublin Institute of Advanced Studies for a translation of a poem from *Irish Bardic Poetry* by Osborn Bergin.

Curtis Brown Ltd, London, on behalf of the Estate of Elizabeth Bowen, and Alfred Knopf Inc., New York, for an extract from 'Summer Night', copyright © 1941, renewed 1969, by Elizabeth Bowen.

Patrick Boyle and Grove Press Inc., New York, for an extract from 'Go Away, Old Man, Go Away' (published in *At Night all Cats are Grey*, MacGibbon and Kee, London, 1966) copyright © Patrick Boyle.

Patricia MacManus for a poem from *The Four Winds of Erin* by Ethna Carbery.

Sheed and Ward Ltd, London, for an extract from *A Little Kept* by Eileen Gormanston.

Colin Smythe Ltd, publishers of the Coole edition of Lady Gregory's works, for her poem 'Donal Oge: Grief of a Girl's Heart'.

W. H. Allen and Co. Ltd, London, and Grove Press Inc., New York, for an extract from *My Life and Loves*, copyright © 1925 by Frank Harris, renewed 1953 by Nellie Harris. Copyright © 1963 by Arthur Leonard Ross as executor of the Frank Harris estate.

Mercier Press, Cork, for lines from two poems in *Love Songs of the Irish* edited by James N. Healy.

University of Minnesota Press, Minneapolis, for an extract from *Anna Livia Plurabelle, The Making of a Chapter* edited by F. H. Higginson, copyright © by the University of Minnesota.

The grandchildren of Douglas Hyde, late President of Ireland, for three poems by Douglas Hyde.

258

The Bodley Head, London, and Random House Inc., New York, for an extract from *Ulysses* by James Joyce, copyright © 1914 and 1918 by Margaret Caroline Anderson, renewed 1942 and 1946 by Nora Joseph Joyce.

Mrs Katharine B. Kavanagh and Martin Brian and O'Keeffe Ltd, London, for a poem from *Collected Poems* by Patrick Kavanagh.

Mercier Press, Cork, for extracts from *Letters of a Matchmaker* and *Letters of a Love-Hungry Farmer* by John B. Keane.

Victor Gollancz Ltd, London, and Curtis Brown Ltd, New York, for an extract from a short story in the collection *A Cow in the House*, copyright © Benedict Kiely 1978.

Faber and Faber Ltd, London, and Little, Brown and Co., Boston, for an extract from a short story in the collection *Nightlines*, copyright © 1970 by John McGahern.

John Montague and Donncha O Corrain for their translation 'The Blameless Lecher' from the medieval Irish.

Brian Moore, Andre Deutsch Ltd, London, and The Viking Press Inc., New York, for an extract from *The Emperor of Ice-Cream* copyright © Brian Moore 1965.

Oxford University Press, Oxford, for three poems from *Early Irish Lyrics*, edited and translated by Gerard Murphy.

Weidenfeld and Nicolson Ltd, London, and Harcourt Brace Jovanovich Inc., New York, for an extract from 'Over' from *A Scandalous Woman and Other Stories* copyright © 1974 by Edna O'Brien; Weidenfeld and Nicolson Ltd, London, and Double-day and Co. Inc., New York, for an extract from *Johnny I hardly knew you* copyright © 1977 by Edna O'Brien.

Hart-Davis MacGibbon Ltd/Granada Publishing Ltd, St Albans, for an extract from *The Poor Mouth* by Flann O'Brien.

Macmillan, London and Basingstoke, and Macmillan Publishing Co. Inc., New York, for an extract from *Inishfallen, Fare Thee Well* by Sean O'Casey, copyright © 1949 by Sean O'Casey, renewed 1977 by Eileen O'Casey, Breon O'Casey and Shivaun O'Casey.

A. D. Peters and Co. Ltd, London, and Joan Daves, New York, for six poems translated by Frank O'Connor.

Pan Books Ltd, London, for two ballads taken from *Irish Street Ballads* and *More Irish Street Ballads* collected and annotated by Colm O Lochlainn.

Cassell Ltd, London, for an extract from *Charles Stewart Parnell* by Katherine O'Shea.

Basil Payne for his poem 'Man and Wife' (published in *Love in the Afternoon*, Gill and Macmillan, Dublin, and Macmillan, London, 1971), copyright © Basil Payne.

Patrick C. Power for an extract from his translation of Egerton MS no. 1782 and his poem 'A Quandary'.

The Society of Authors on behalf of the Bernard Shaw Estate for two letters from *Bernard Shaw: Collected Letters 1874–97* edited by Dan H. Lawrence (Max Reinhardt Ltd, London, 1965).

Sir Patrick Coghill and Chatto and Windus, London, for an extract from *The Real Charlotte* by E. Œ. Somerville and Martin Ross.

The Society of Authors as the literary representative of the Estate of James Stephens for extracts from *Deirdre* (Macmillan, London, 1923), *Here are Ladies* (Macmillan, London, 1913, copyright renewed 1941 by James Stephens) and *Etched in Moonlight* (Macmillan, London, 1928).

George Allen and Unwin Ltd, London, and Random House Inc., New York, for an extract from *The Playboy of the Western World* and the short story 'He That's Dead Can Do No Hurt' copyright © 1907 by J. M. Synge; the Belknap Press of Harvard University Press, Cambridge, Mass., for two letters from *Letters to Molly: John Millington Synge to Maire O'Neill* 1906–1909 edited by Ann Saddlemyer, copyright © 1971 by Ann Saddlemyer.

The Society of Authors and Miss Pamela Hinkson for a poem by Katharine Tynan Hinkson.

The Estate of Vyvyan Holland for a letter from Oscar Wilde to his wife.

M. B. Yeats, Miss Anne Yeats, Macmillan, London and Basingstoke, and Macmillan Publishing Co. Inc., New York, for an extract from *Autobiography* by W. B. Yeats and two poems from *Collected Poems* by W. B. Yeats, copyright © 1919 by Macmillan Publishing Co. Inc., renewed 1947 by Bertha Georgie Yeats.

LIST OF AUTHORS AND TITLES